the life-changing *manga* of tidying up

a magical story

marie kondo

author of *the life-changing magic of tidying up*

———

illustrated by yuko uramoto
translated from the japanese by cathy hirano

TEN SPEED PRESS
California | New York

the life-changing *manga* of

contents

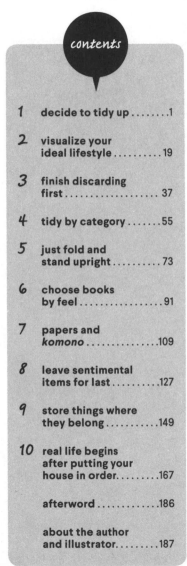

Chiaki Suzuki

Twenty-nine years old. Sales
rep. Single. Falls in love easily
but loses interest quickly,
which makes it hard for her to
have a lasting relationship.

tidying up — *a magical story*

introducing the characters

Marie Kondo

Tidying consultant. Nickname: KonMari. Has a winning smile but is an exacting instructor.

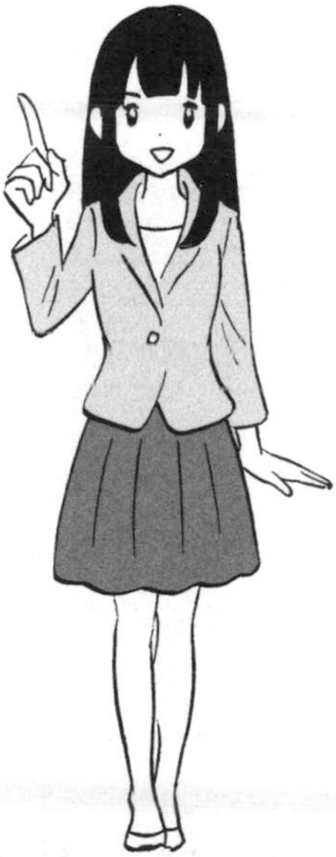

Chiaki's Neighbor

Good-looking guy who lives in the apartment next to Chiaki's. Works as a cook at a café. Likes to keep things tidy.

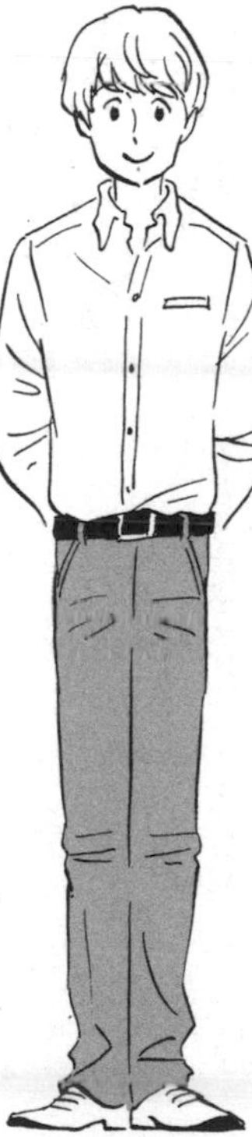

You really want to tidy up, but you don't believe you can. If this describes you, don't worry. You, too, can be just like Chiaki in this story.

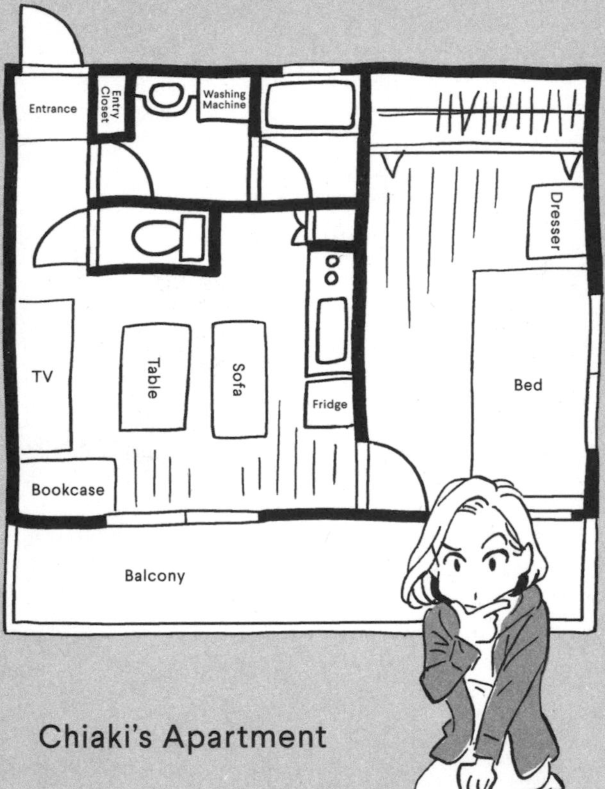
Entrance
Entry Closet
Washing Machine
Dresser
TV
Table
Sofa
Fridge
Bed
Bookcase
Balcony

Chiaki's Apartment

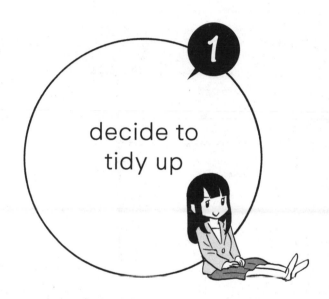

1

decide to tidy up

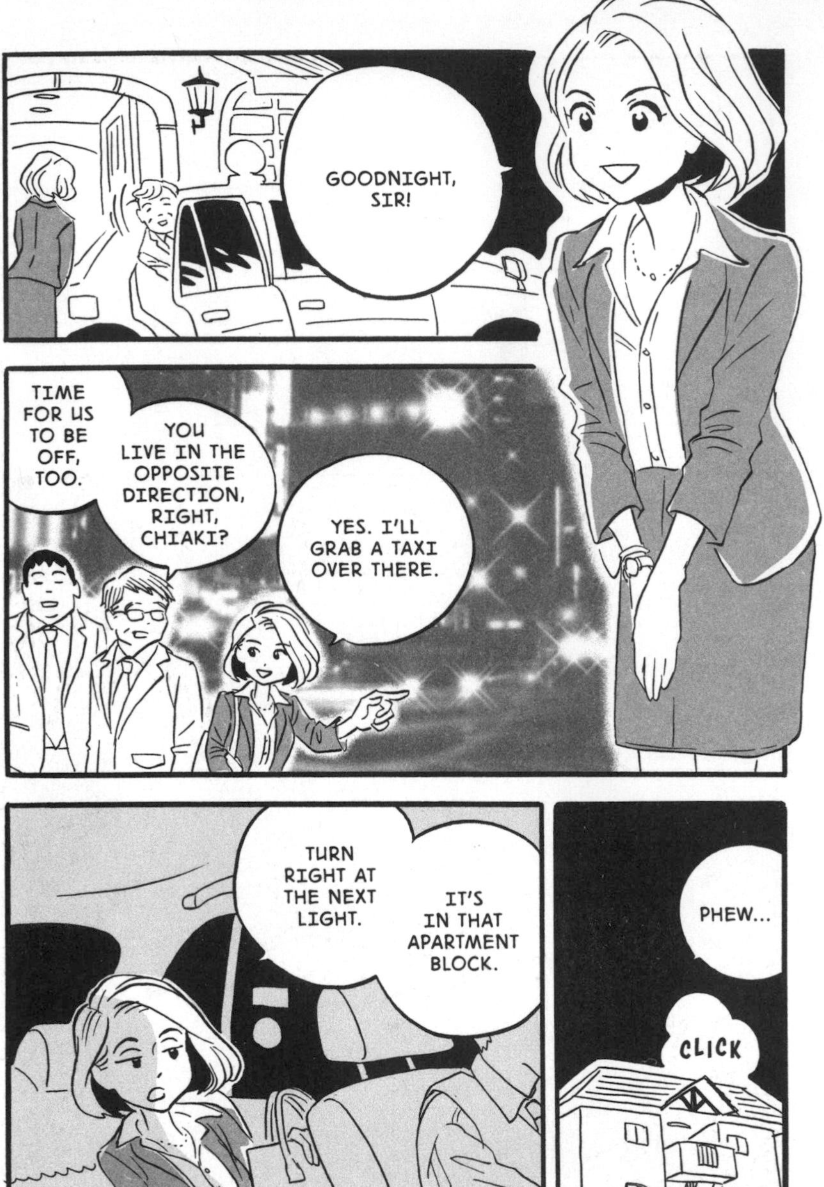
GOODNIGHT, SIR!
TIME FOR US TO BE OFF, TOO.
YOU LIVE IN THE OPPOSITE DIRECTION, RIGHT, CHIAKI?
YES. I'LL GRAB A TAXI OVER THERE.
TURN RIGHT AT THE NEXT LIGHT.
IT'S IN THAT APARTMENT BLOCK.
PHEW...
CLICK

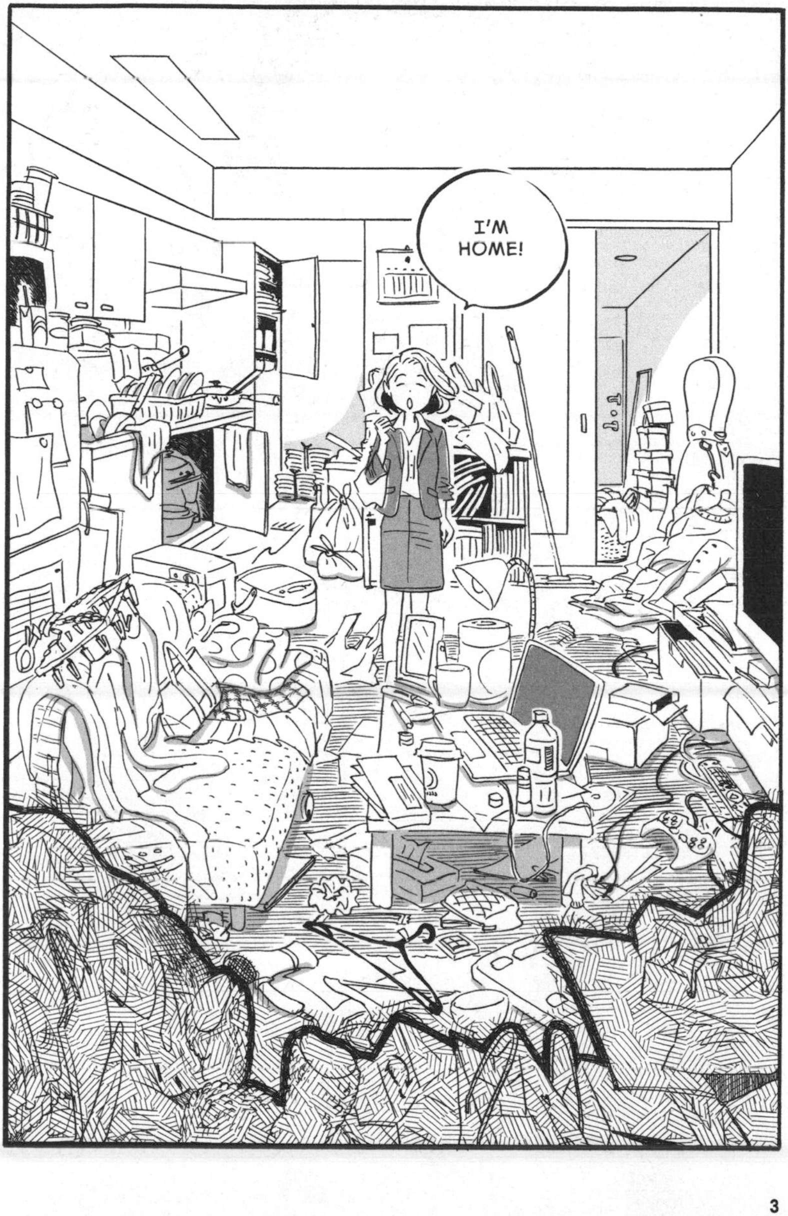
I'M HOME!

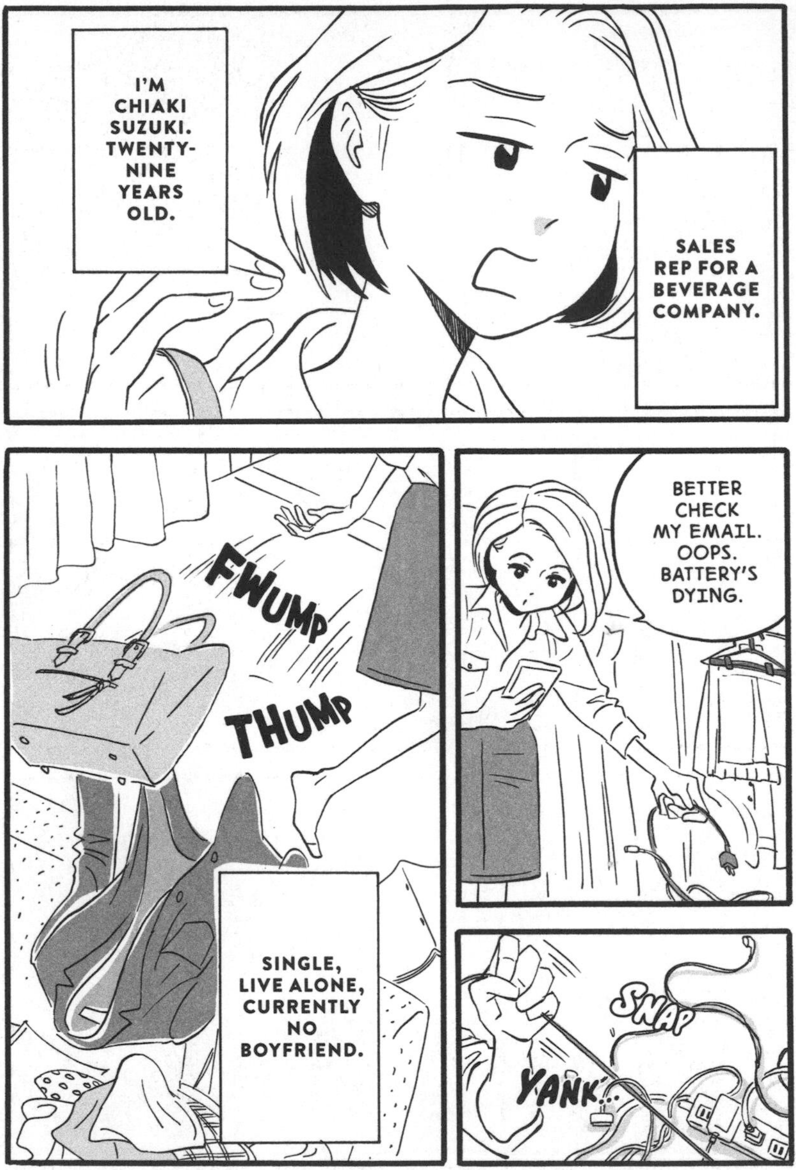
I'M CHIAKI SUZUKI. TWENTY-NINE YEARS OLD.
SALES REP FOR A BEVERAGE COMPANY.
FWUMP
THUMP
SINGLE, LIVE ALONE, CURRENTLY NO BOYFRIEND.
BETTER CHECK MY EMAIL. OOPS. BATTERY'S DYING.
SNAP
YANK...

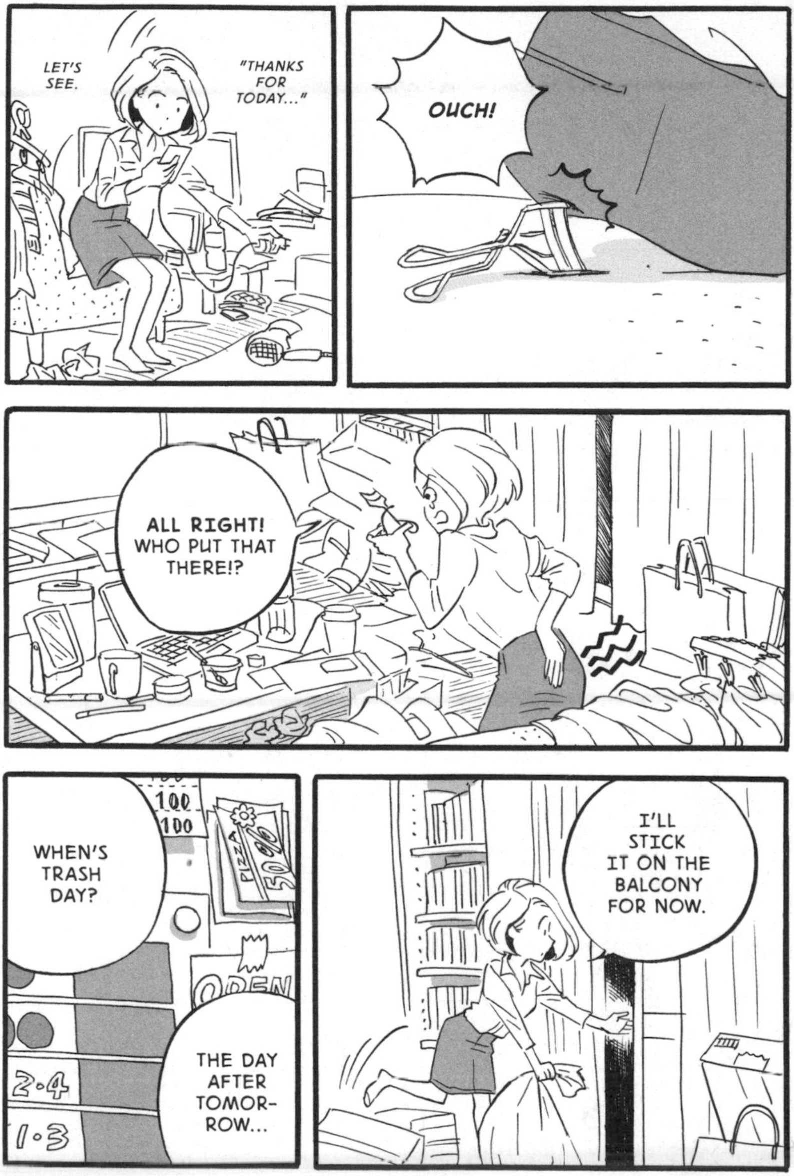
LET'S SEE.
"THANKS FOR TODAY..."
OUCH!
ALL RIGHT! WHO PUT THAT THERE!?
100
100
100
PIZZA
50%
OPEN
2·4
1·3
WHEN'S TRASH DAY?
THE DAY AFTER TOMOR-ROW...
I'LL STICK IT ON THE BALCONY FOR NOW.

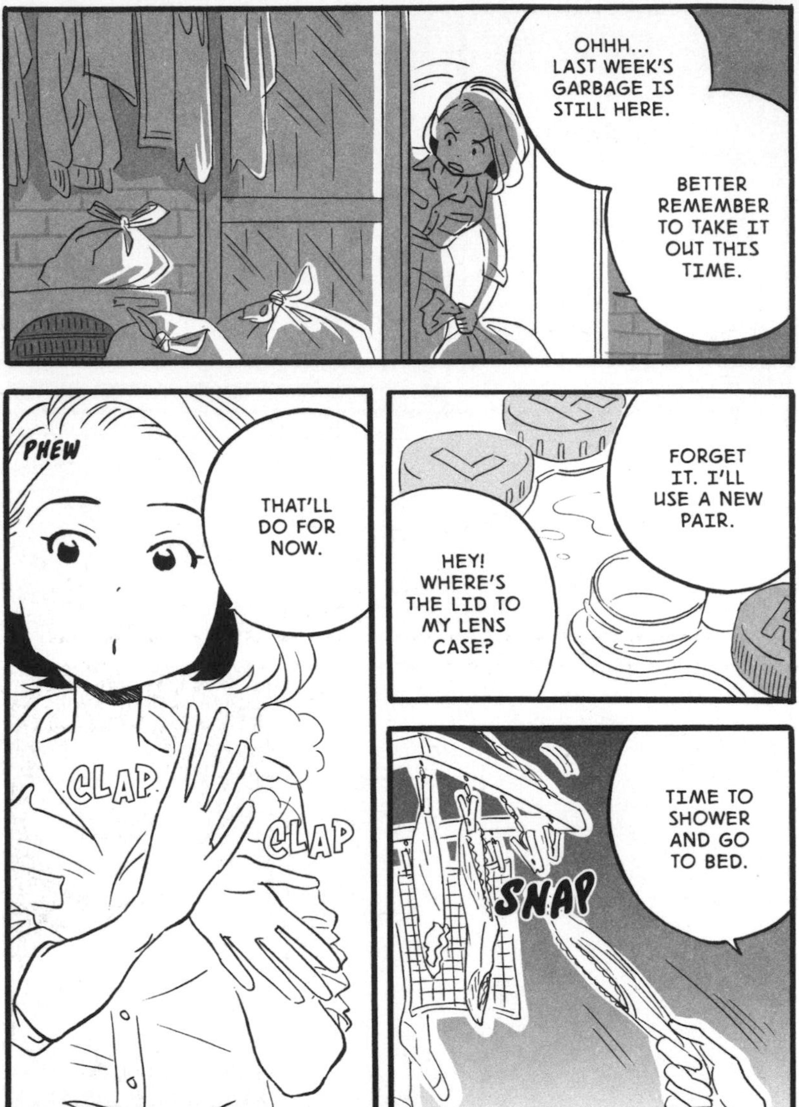
OHHH... LAST WEEK'S GARBAGE IS STILL HERE.
BETTER REMEMBER TO TAKE IT OUT THIS TIME.
PHEW
THAT'LL DO FOR NOW.
CLAP
CLAP
HEY! WHERE'S THE LID TO MY LENS CASE?
FORGET IT. I'LL USE A NEW PAIR.
SNAP
TIME TO SHOWER AND GO TO BED.

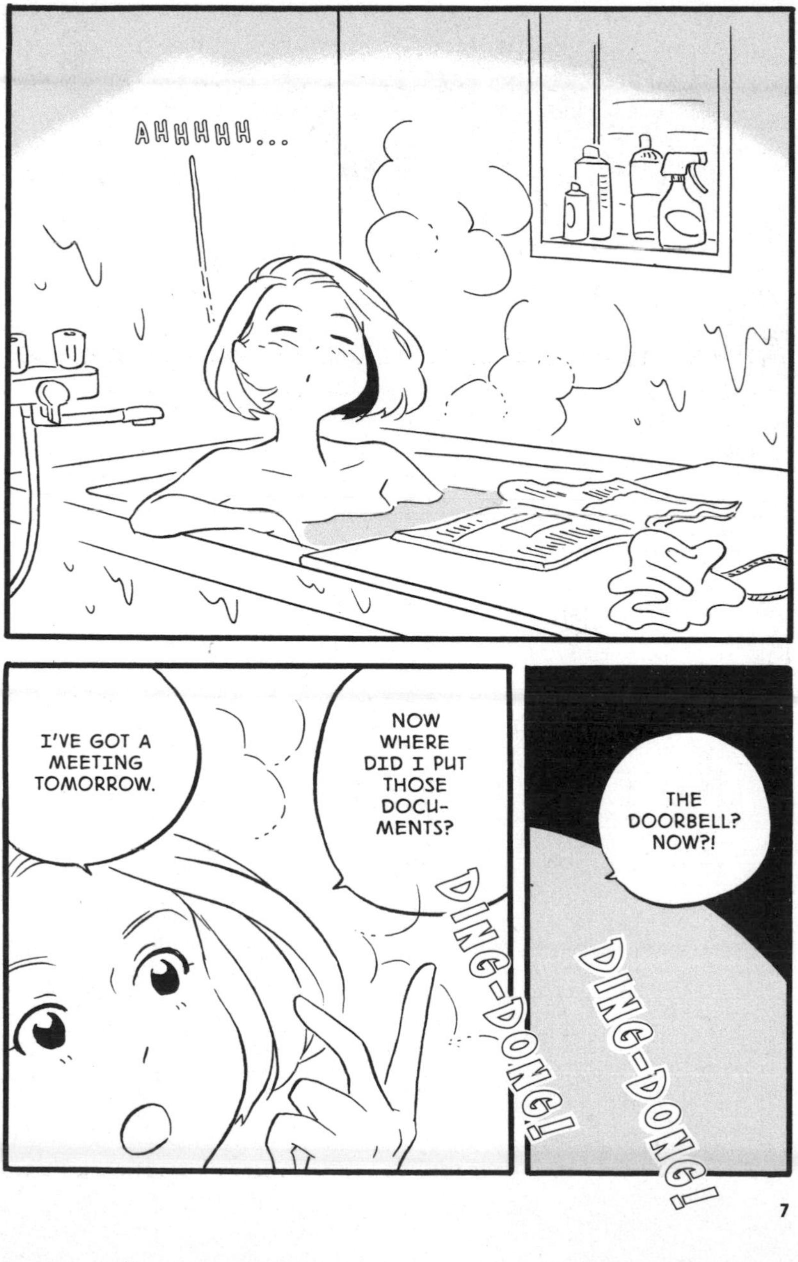
AHHHHH...
I'VE GOT A MEETING TOMORROW.
NOW WHERE DID I PUT THOSE DOCU-MENTS?
DING-DONG!
THE DOORBELL? NOW?!
DING-DONG!

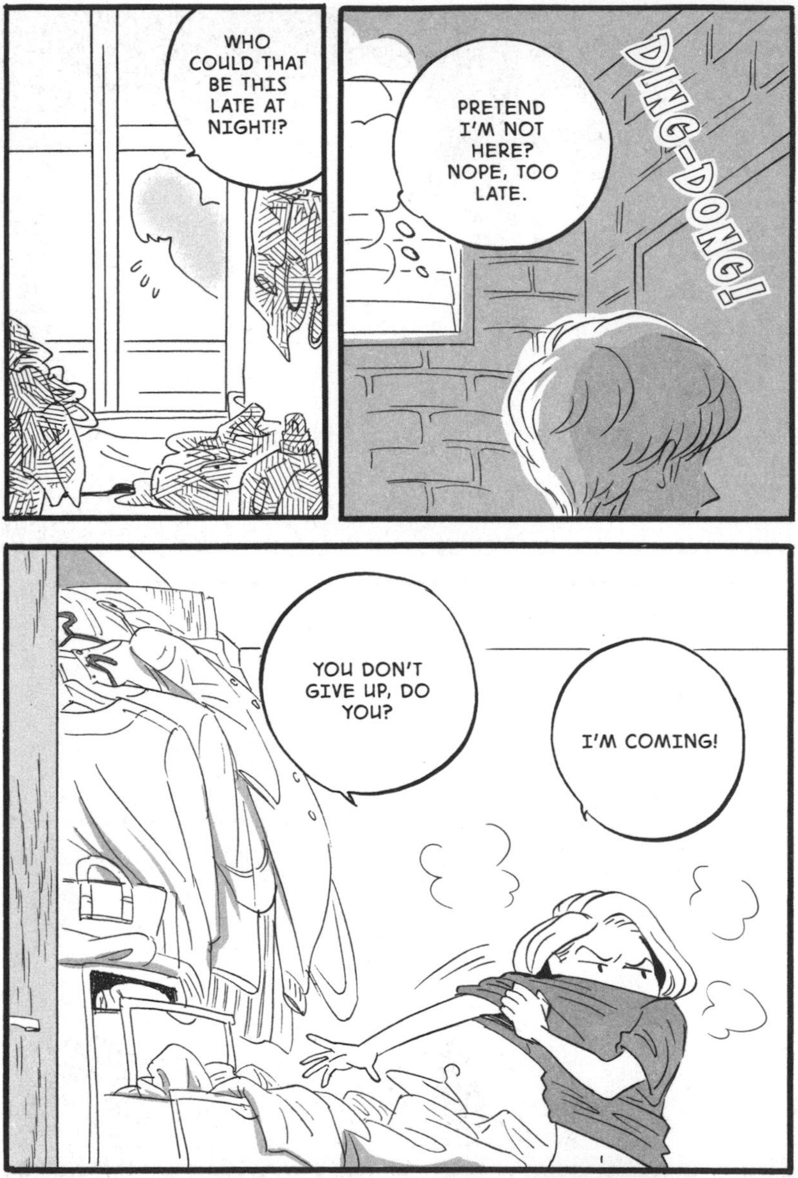
WHO COULD THAT BE THIS LATE AT NIGHT!?
PRETEND I'M NOT HERE? NOPE, TOO LATE.
DING-DONG!
YOU DON'T GIVE UP, DO YOU?
I'M COMING!

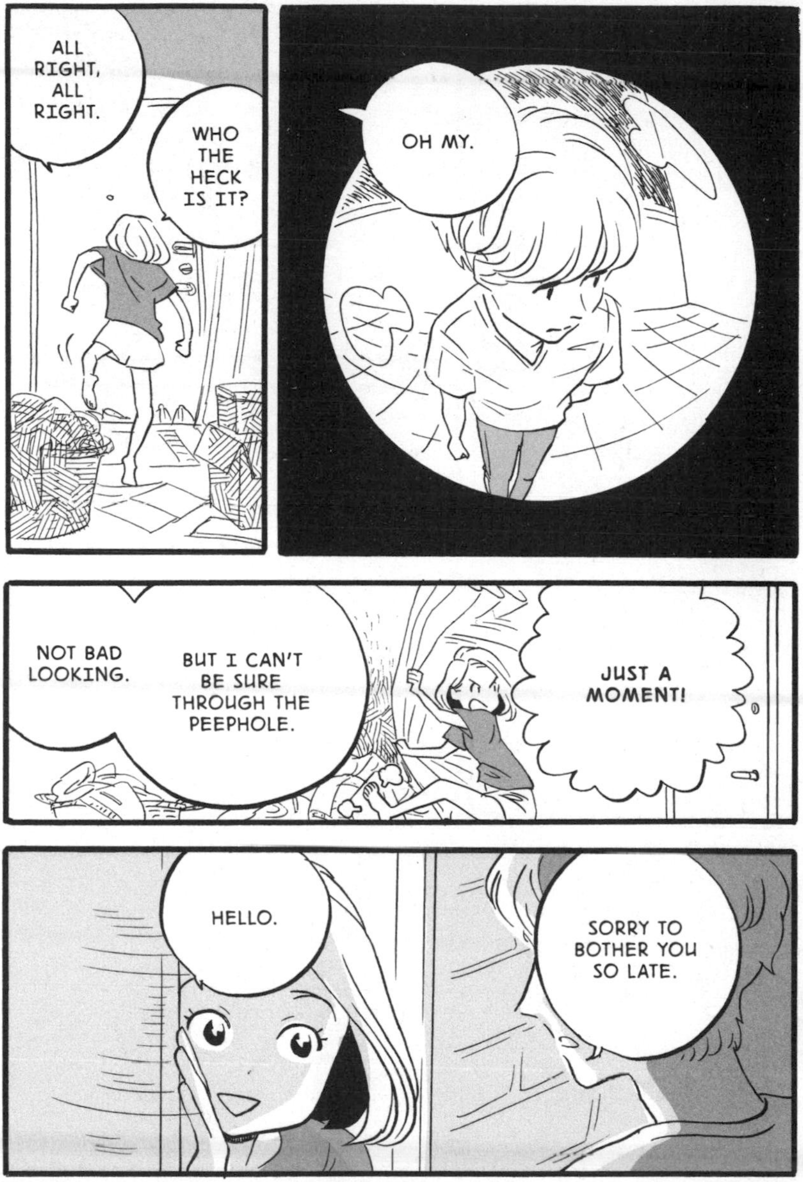
ALL RIGHT, ALL RIGHT.
WHO THE HECK IS IT?
OH MY.
NOT BAD LOOKING.
BUT I CAN'T BE SURE THROUGH THE PEEPHOLE.
JUST A MOMENT!
HELLO.
SORRY TO BOTHER YOU SO LATE.

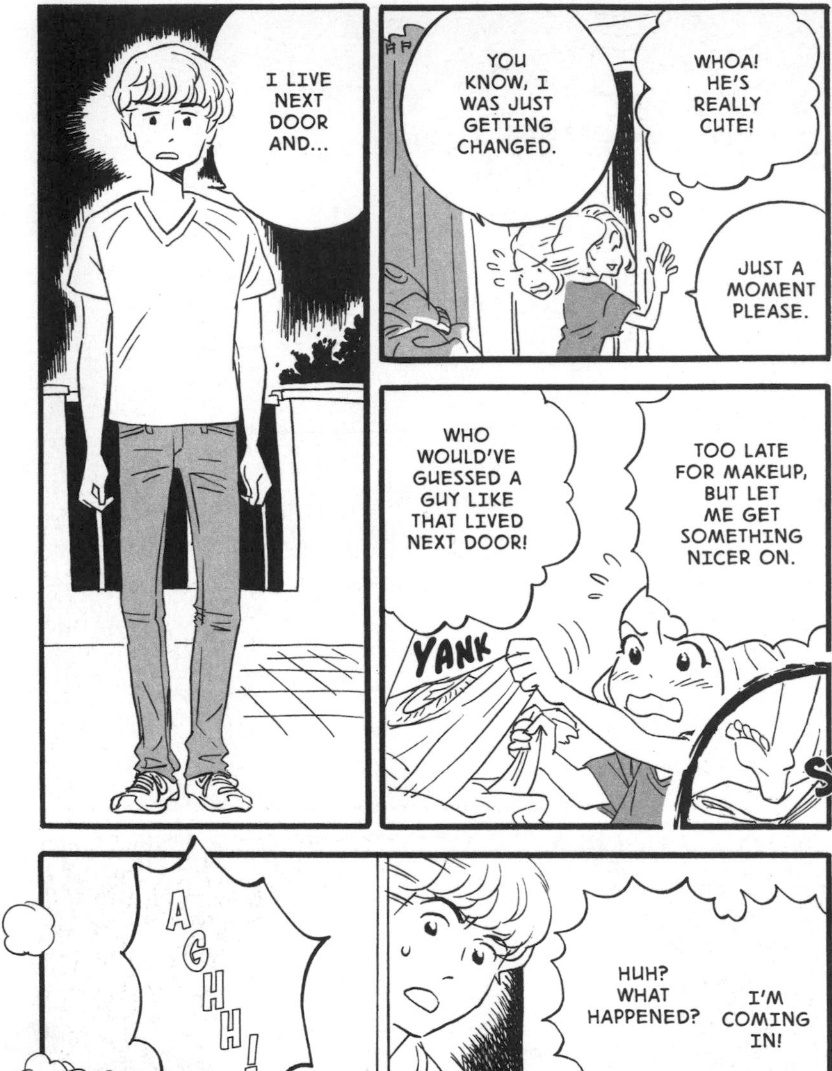
I LIVE NEXT DOOR AND...
YOU KNOW, I WAS JUST GETTING CHANGED.
WHOA! HE'S REALLY CUTE!
JUST A MOMENT PLEASE.
WHO WOULD'VE GUESSED A GUY LIKE THAT LIVED NEXT DOOR!
TOO LATE FOR MAKEUP, BUT LET ME GET SOMETHING NICER ON.
YANK
SLIP
AGHH!
BUMP-BUMP
THUD!
HUH? WHAT HAPPENED?
I'M COMING IN!

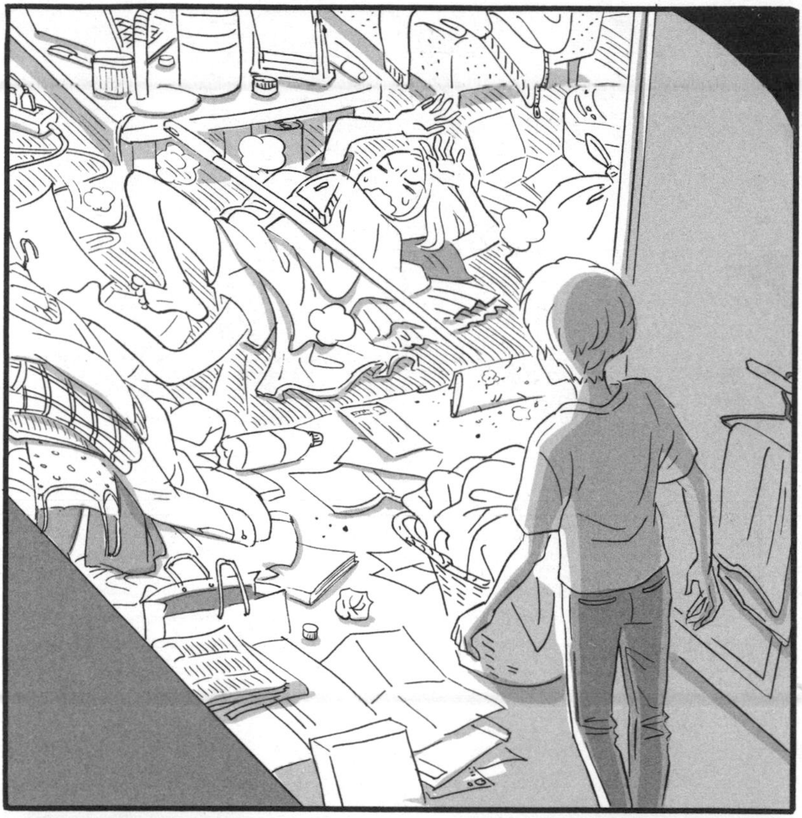

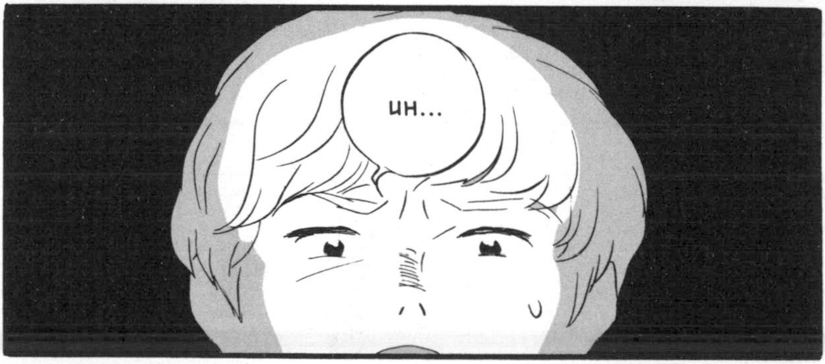
UH...

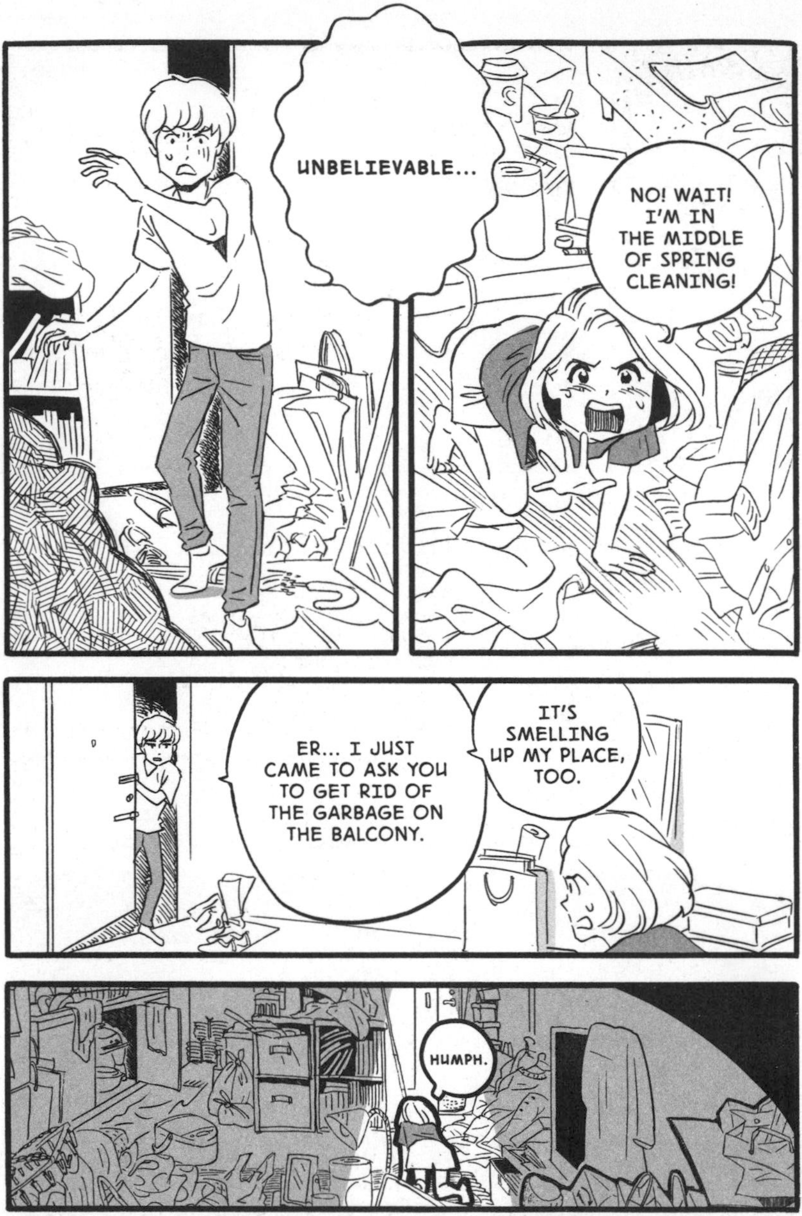
UNBELIEVABLE...
NO! WAIT! I'M IN THE MIDDLE OF SPRING CLEANING!
ER... I JUST CAME TO ASK YOU TO GET RID OF THE GARBAGE ON THE BALCONY.
IT'S SMELLING UP MY PLACE, TOO.
HUMPH.

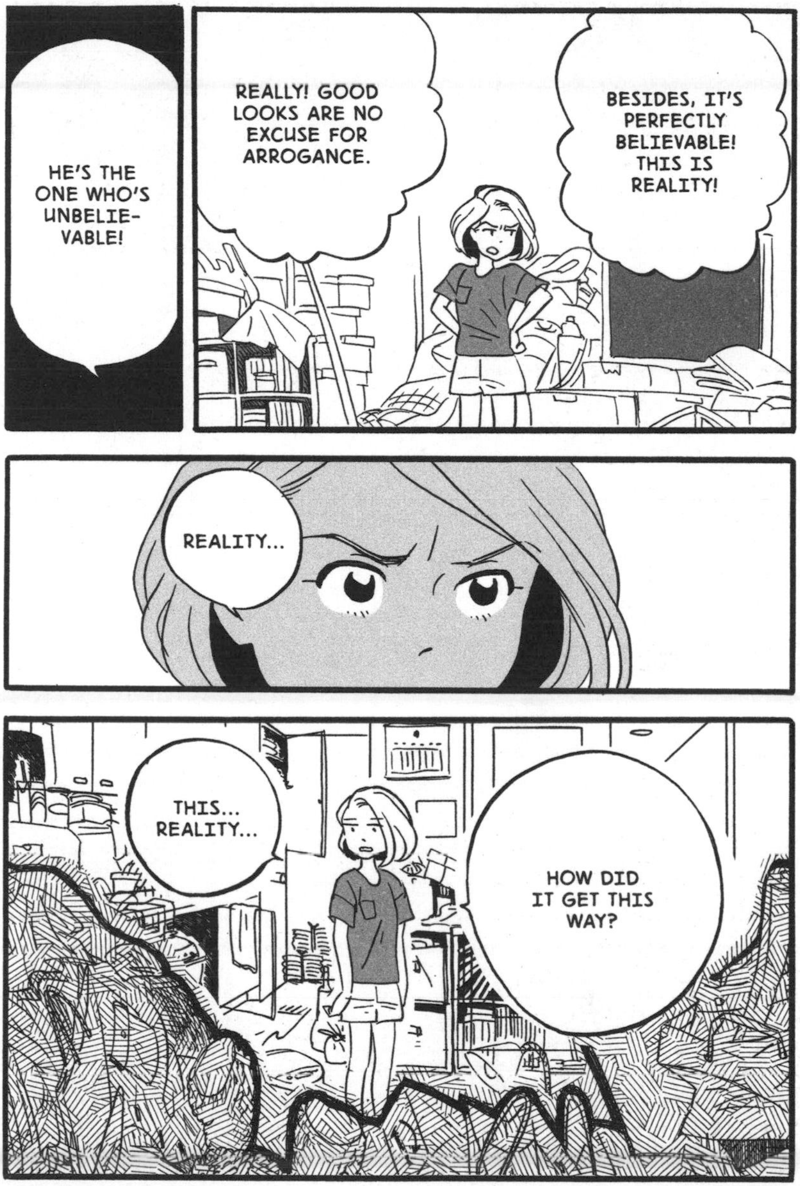
HE'S THE ONE WHO'S UNBELIE-VABLE!
REALLY! GOOD LOOKS ARE NO EXCUSE FOR ARROGANCE.
BESIDES, IT'S PERFECTLY BELIEVABLE! THIS IS REALITY!
REALITY...
THIS... REALITY...
HOW DID IT GET THIS WAY?

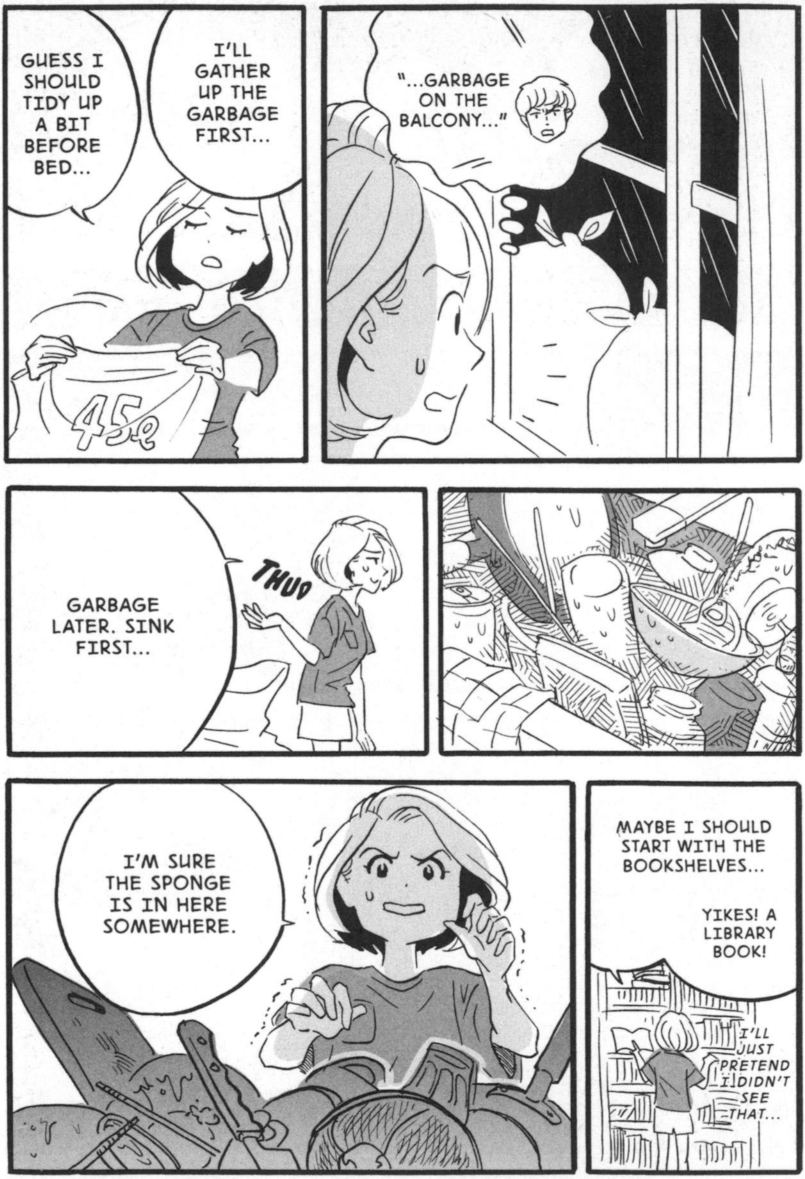
GUESS I SHOULD TIDY UP A BIT BEFORE BED...
I'LL GATHER UP THE GARBAGE FIRST...
45ℓ
"...GARBAGE ON THE BALCONY..."
GARBAGE LATER. SINK FIRST...
THUD
I'M SURE THE SPONGE IS IN HERE SOMEWHERE.
MAYBE I SHOULD START WITH THE BOOKSHELVES...
YIKES! A LIBRARY BOOK!
I'LL JUST PRETEND I DIDN'T SEE THAT...

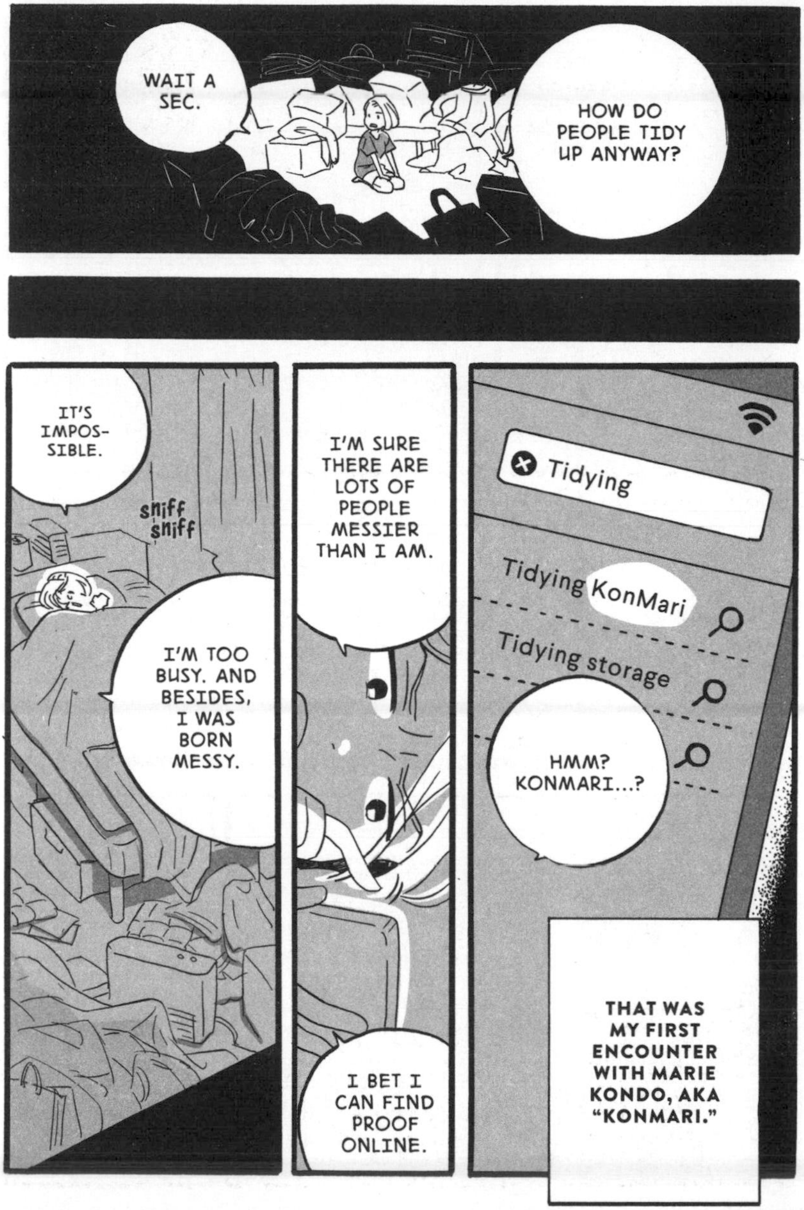
WAIT A SEC.
HOW DO PEOPLE TIDY UP ANYWAY?
IT'S IMPOS-SIBLE.
sniff sniff
I'M TOO BUSY. AND BESIDES, I WAS BORN MESSY.
I'M SURE THERE ARE LOTS OF PEOPLE MESSIER THAN I AM.
I BET I CAN FIND PROOF ONLINE.
Tidying
Tidying KonMari
Tidying storage
HMM? KONMARI...?
THAT WAS MY FIRST ENCOUNTER WITH MARIE KONDO, AKA "KONMARI."

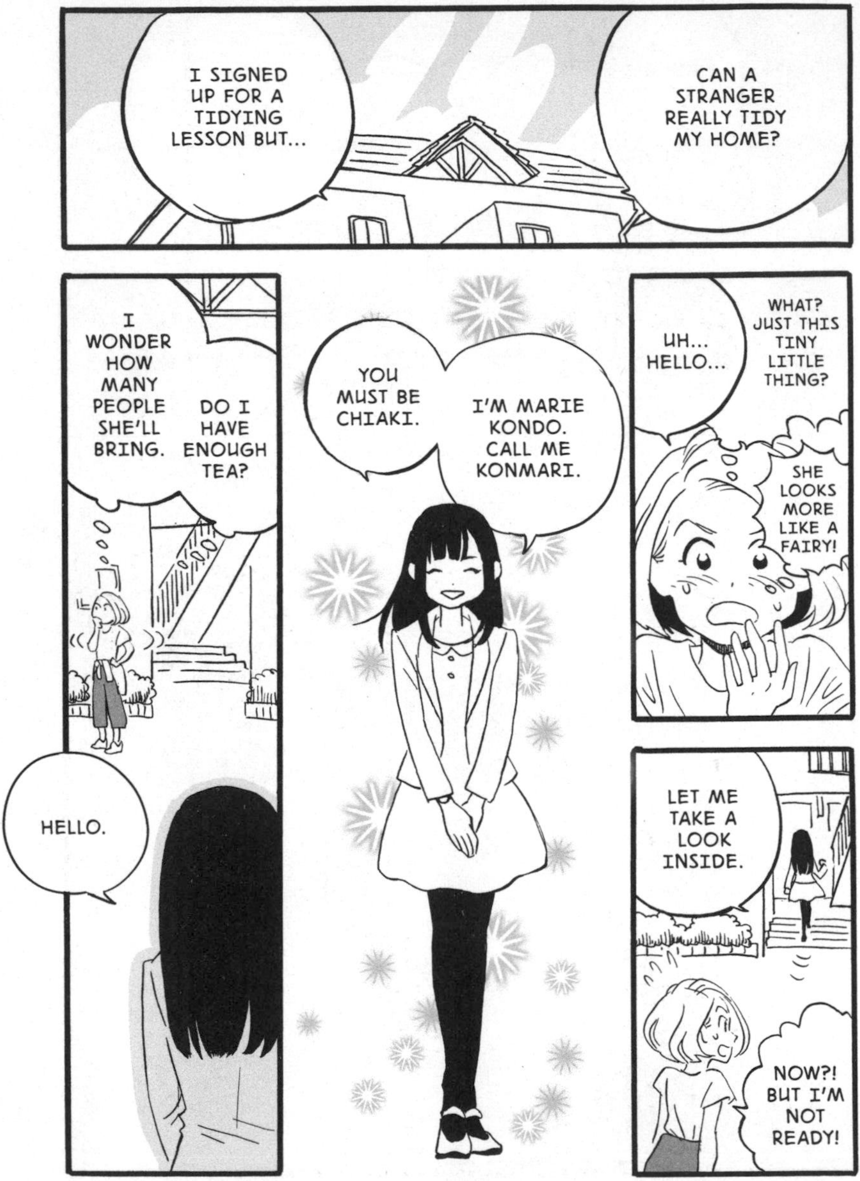
I SIGNED UP FOR A TIDYING LESSON BUT...
CAN A STRANGER REALLY TIDY MY HOME?
I WONDER HOW MANY PEOPLE SHE'LL BRING.
DO I HAVE ENOUGH TEA?
HELLO.
YOU MUST BE CHIAKI.
I'M MARIE KONDO. CALL ME KONMARI.
UH... HELLO...
WHAT? JUST THIS TINY LITTLE THING?
SHE LOOKS MORE LIKE A FAIRY!
LET ME TAKE A LOOK INSIDE.
NOW?! BUT I'M NOT READY!

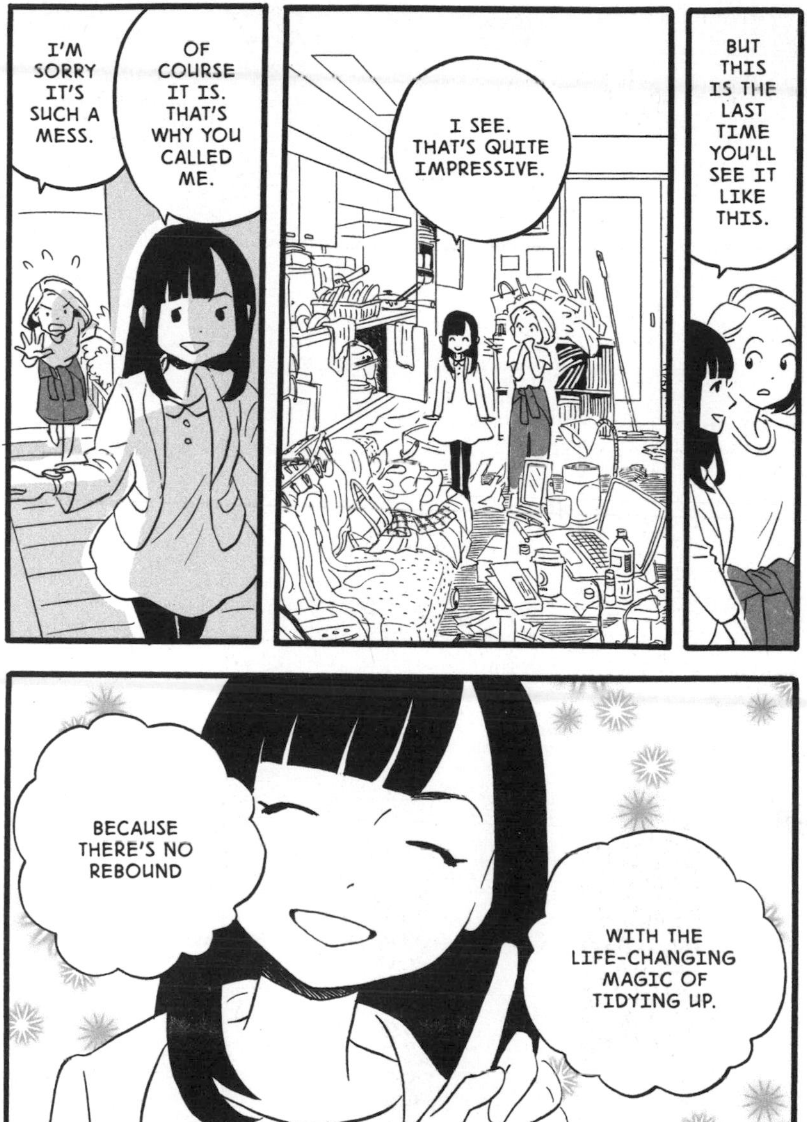
I'M SORRY IT'S SUCH A MESS.
OF COURSE IT IS. THAT'S WHY YOU CALLED ME.
I SEE. THAT'S QUITE IMPRESSIVE.
BUT THIS IS THE LAST TIME YOU'LL SEE IT LIKE THIS.
BECAUSE THERE'S NO REBOUND
WITH THE LIFE-CHANGING MAGIC OF TIDYING UP.

Think you can't do it? If so, you're wrong. Everyone can learn how to tidy up.

———

Success in tidying depends 90 percent on your mind-set. Of course, know-how is important, too, but the chances of a rebound are higher if you only learn the "how-to's" of tidying.

The approach that you are about to start is not simply about decluttering your home or making it look neat when visitors drop in. Instead, it will change your whole life and fill it with joy.

Start by believing with all your heart that you can and will be tidy.

2

visualize
your ideal
lifestyle

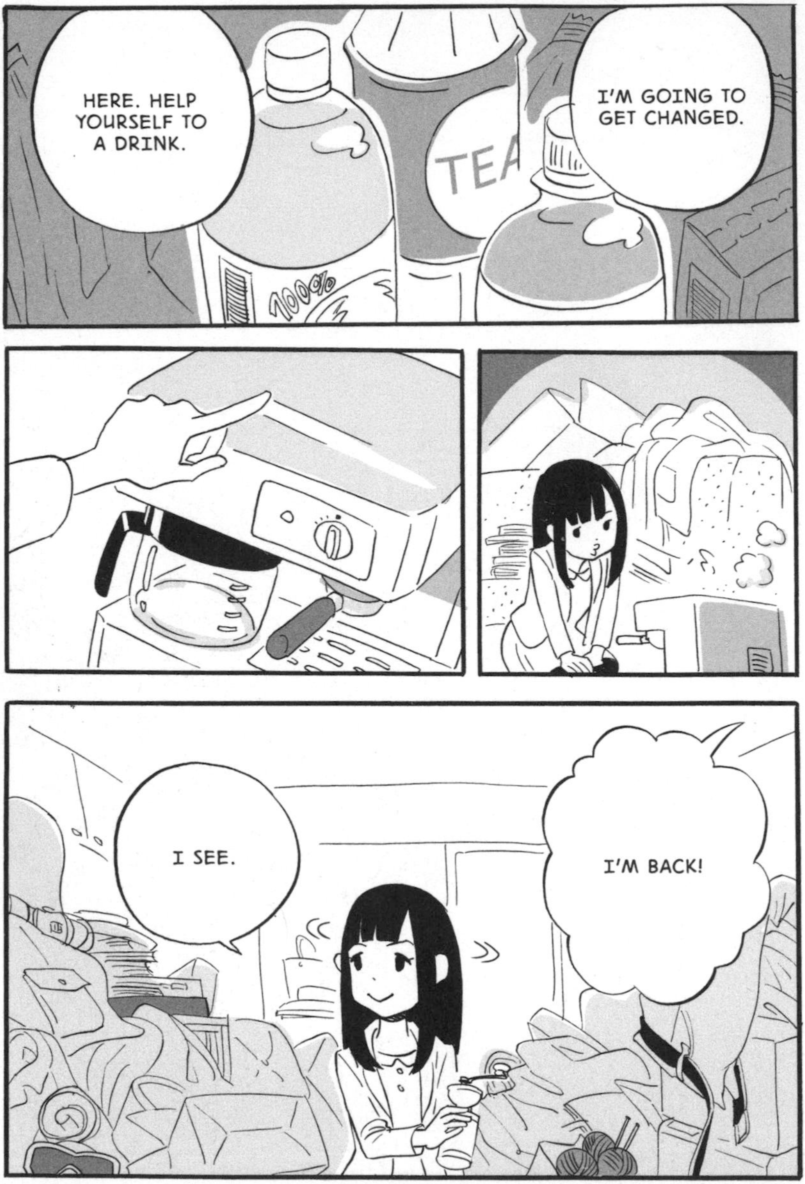
HERE. HELP YOURSELF TO A DRINK.
TEA
100%
I'M GOING TO GET CHANGED.
I SEE.
I'M BACK!

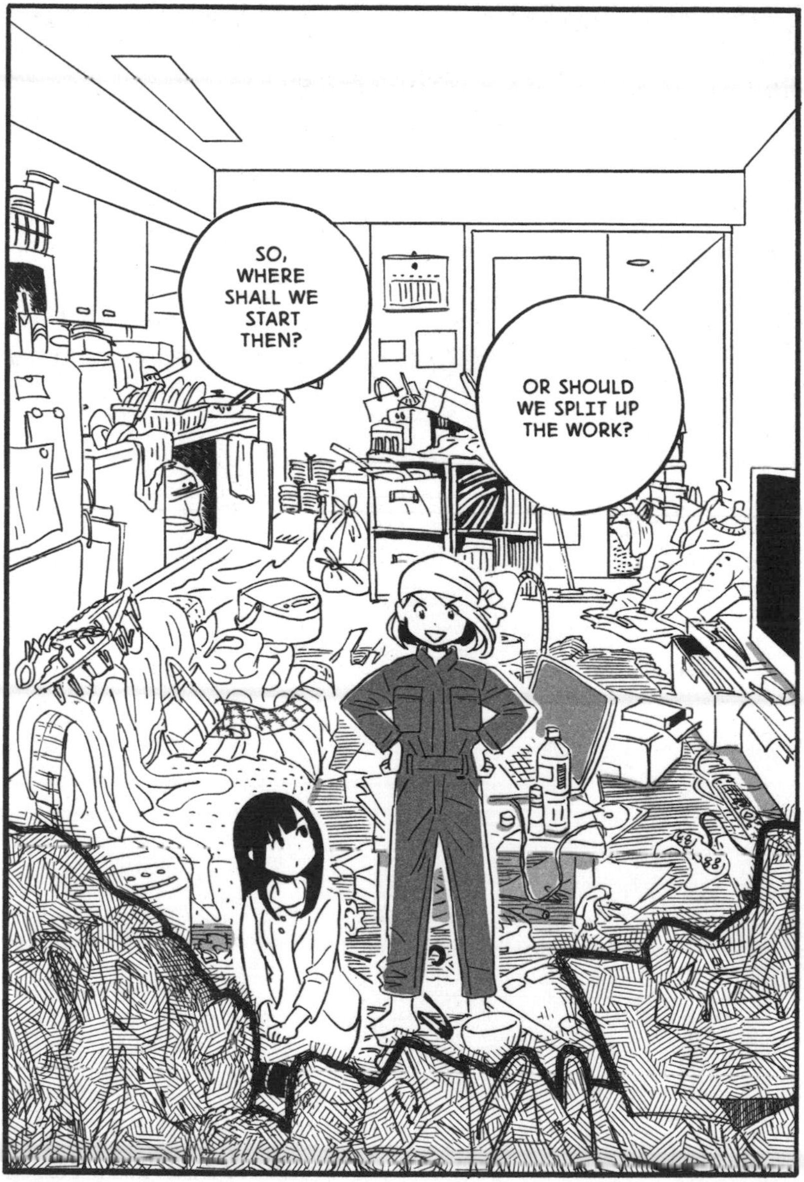
SO, WHERE SHALL WE START THEN?
OR SHOULD WE SPLIT UP THE WORK?

OH, WAIT. DO YOU WANT TO GET CHANGED, TOO?

CHIAKI, PLEASE RELAX.

LET'S HAVE SOME COFFEE.

I LOVE YOUR ESPRESSO MACHINE.

WHAT ...?

AND LOOK AT THESE GORGEOUS CUPS!

Pluck

COFFEE

YOU REALLY LIKE COFFEE, DON'T YOU?

WELL...I USED TO BE REALLY INTO IT.

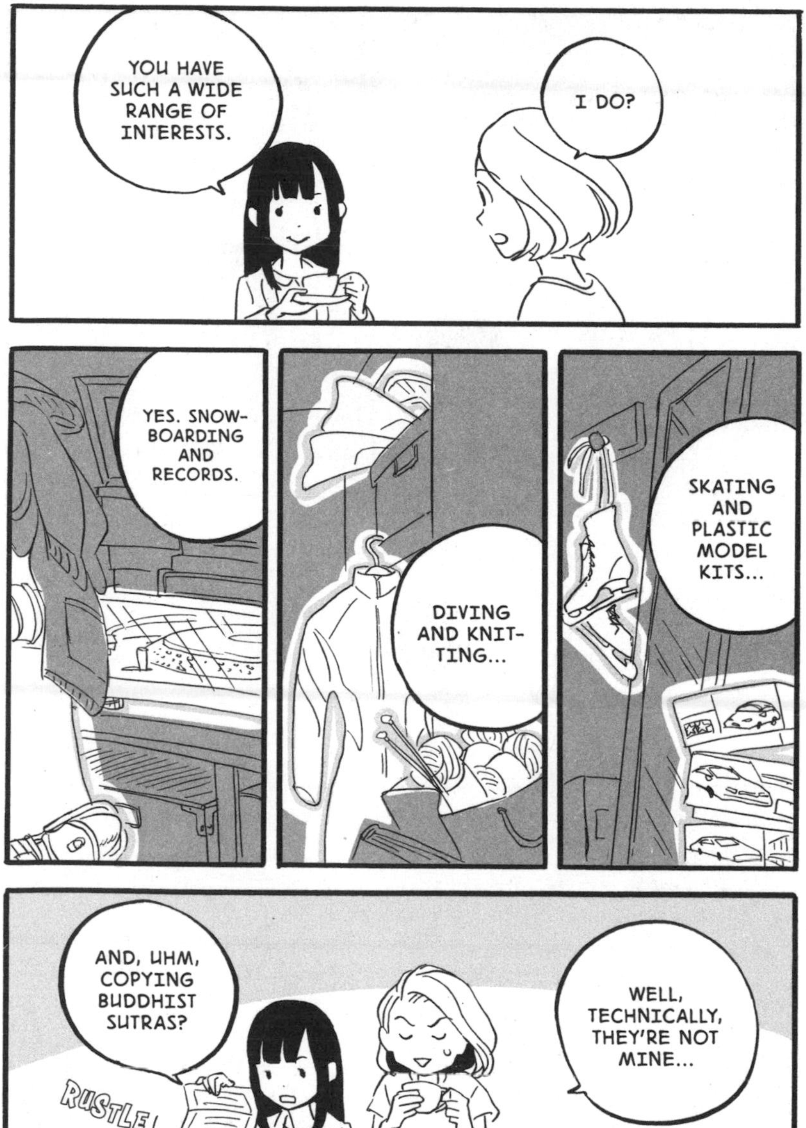
YOU HAVE SUCH A WIDE RANGE OF INTERESTS.
I DO?
YES. SNOW-BOARDING AND RECORDS.
DIVING AND KNIT-TING...
SKATING AND PLASTIC MODEL KITS...
AND, UHM, COPYING BUDDHIST SUTRAS?
RUSTLE
WELL, TECHNICALLY, THEY'RE NOT MINE...

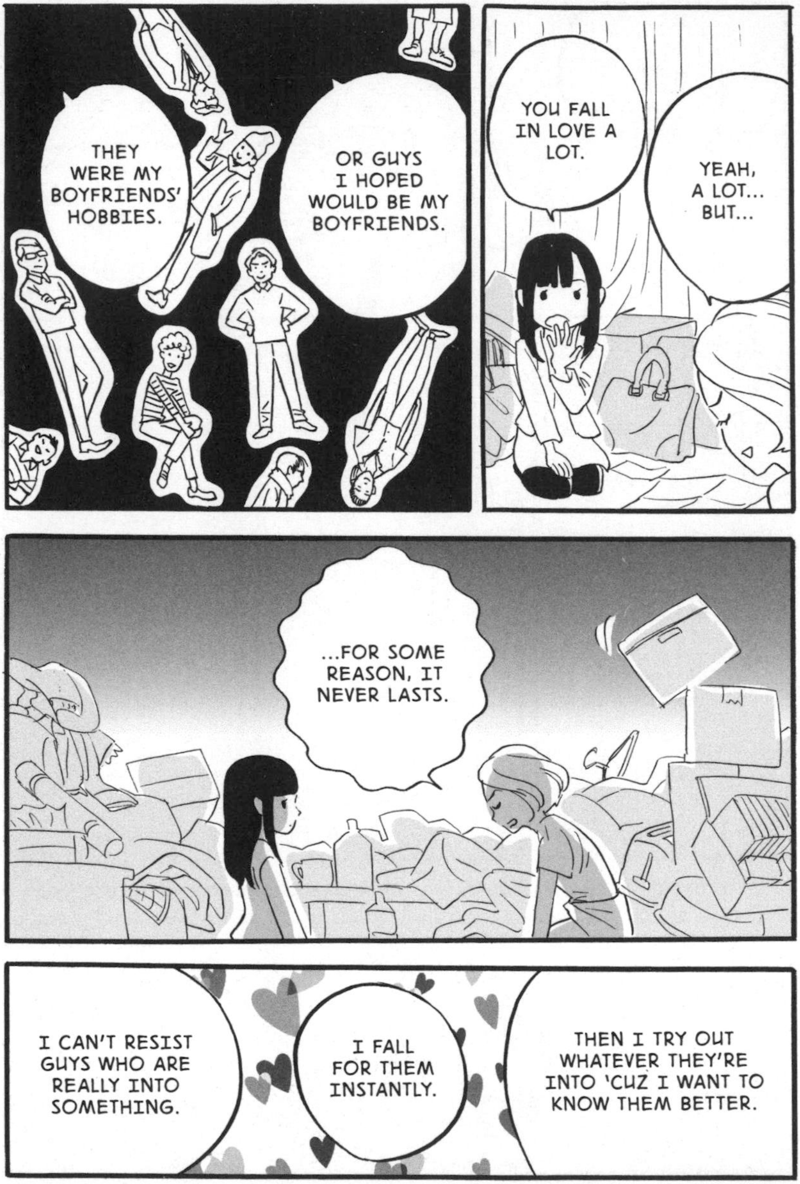
THEY WERE MY BOYFRIENDS' HOBBIES.
OR GUYS I HOPED WOULD BE MY BOYFRIENDS.
YOU FALL IN LOVE A LOT.
YEAH, A LOT... BUT...
...FOR SOME REASON, IT NEVER LASTS.
I CAN'T RESIST GUYS WHO ARE REALLY INTO SOMETHING.
I FALL FOR THEM INSTANTLY.
THEN I TRY OUT WHATEVER THEY'RE INTO 'CUZ I WANT TO KNOW THEM BETTER.

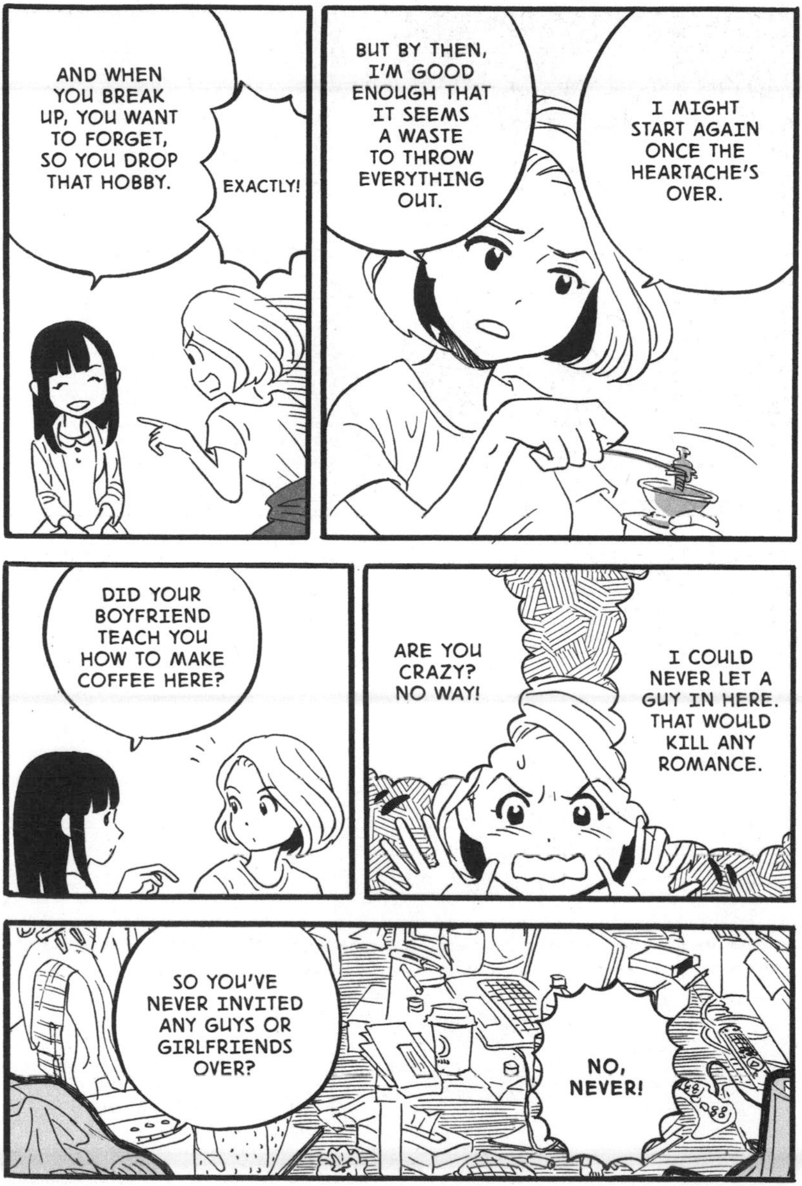
AND WHEN YOU BREAK UP, YOU WANT TO FORGET, SO YOU DROP THAT HOBBY.
EXACTLY!
BUT BY THEN, I'M GOOD ENOUGH THAT IT SEEMS A WASTE TO THROW EVERYTHING OUT.
I MIGHT START AGAIN ONCE THE HEARTACHE'S OVER.
DID YOUR BOYFRIEND TEACH YOU HOW TO MAKE COFFEE HERE?
ARE YOU CRAZY? NO WAY!
I COULD NEVER LET A GUY IN HERE. THAT WOULD KILL ANY ROMANCE.
SO YOU'VE NEVER INVITED ANY GUYS OR GIRLFRIENDS OVER?
NO, NEVER!

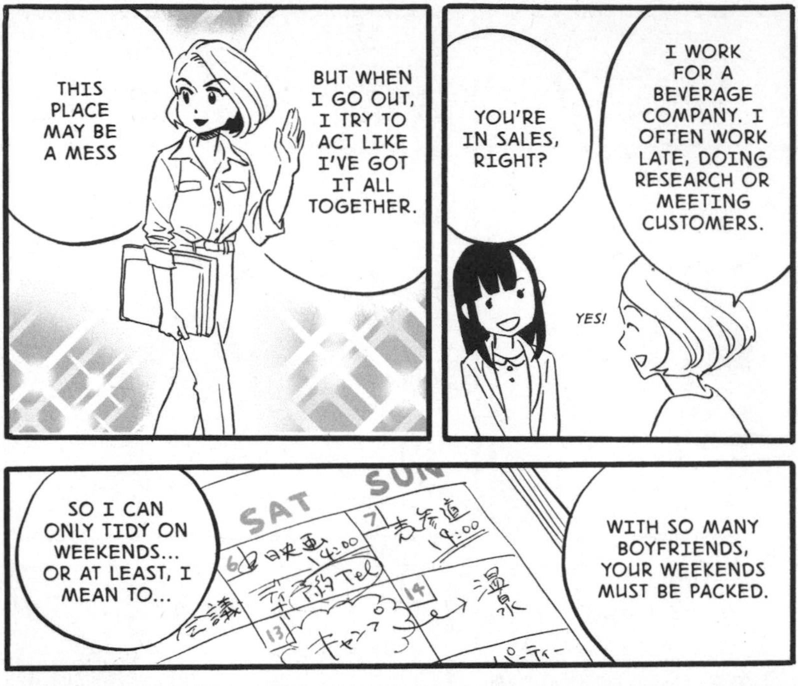
THIS PLACE MAY BE A MESS
BUT WHEN I GO OUT, I TRY TO ACT LIKE I'VE GOT IT ALL TOGETHER.
YOU'RE IN SALES, RIGHT?
YES!
I WORK FOR A BEVERAGE COMPANY. I OFTEN WORK LATE, DOING RESEARCH OR MEETING CUSTOMERS.
SO I CAN ONLY TIDY ON WEEKENDS... OR AT LEAST, I MEAN TO...
SAT
SUN
WITH SO MANY BOYFRIENDS, YOUR WEEKENDS MUST BE PACKED.
MAYBE I'M GREEDY TO WANT BOTH A CAREER AND A LOVE LIFE.
SIGH

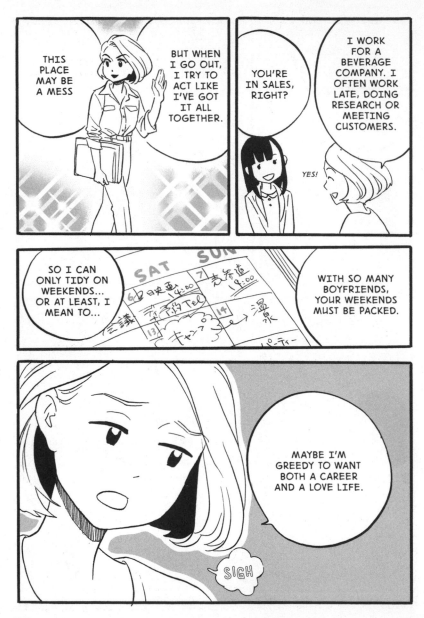

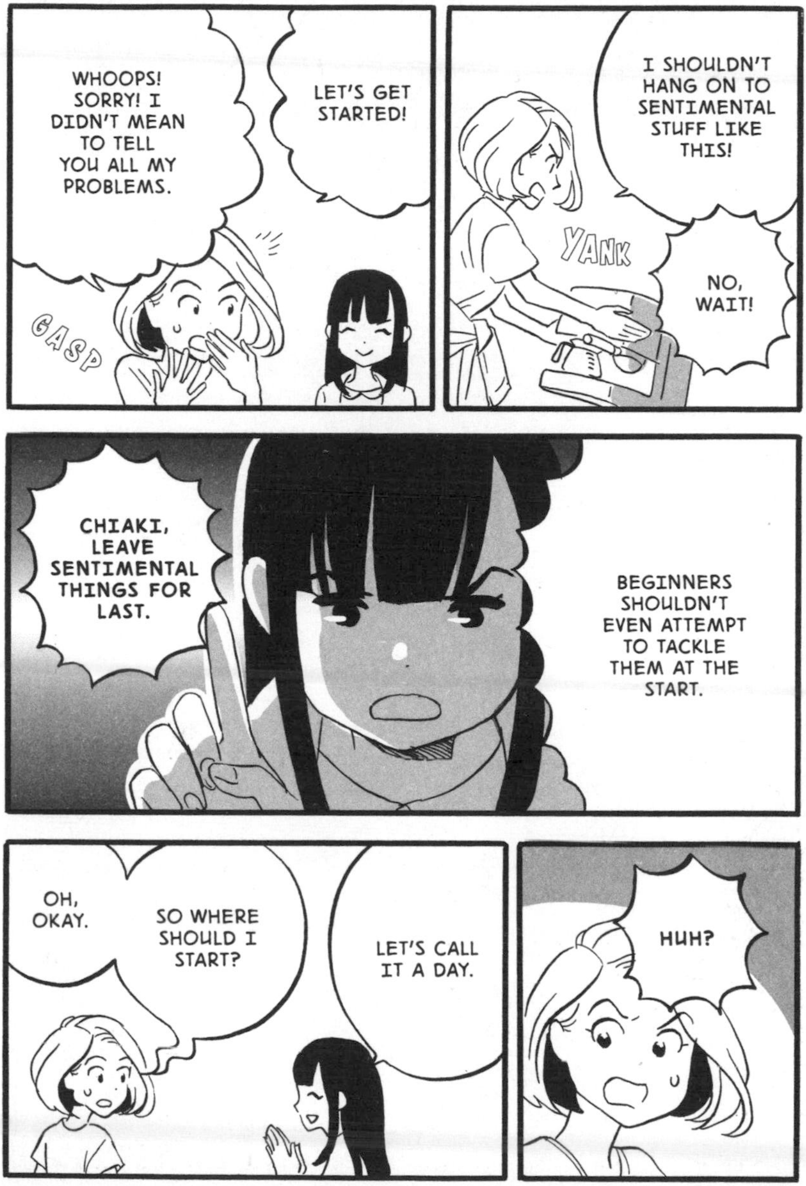
WHOOPS! SORRY! I DIDN'T MEAN TO TELL YOU ALL MY PROBLEMS.
GASP
LET'S GET STARTED!
I SHOULDN'T HANG ON TO SENTIMENTAL STUFF LIKE THIS!
YANK
NO, WAIT!
CHIAKI, LEAVE SENTIMENTAL THINGS FOR LAST.
BEGINNERS SHOULDN'T EVEN ATTEMPT TO TACKLE THEM AT THE START.
OH, OKAY.
SO WHERE SHOULD I START?
LET'S CALL IT A DAY.
HUH?

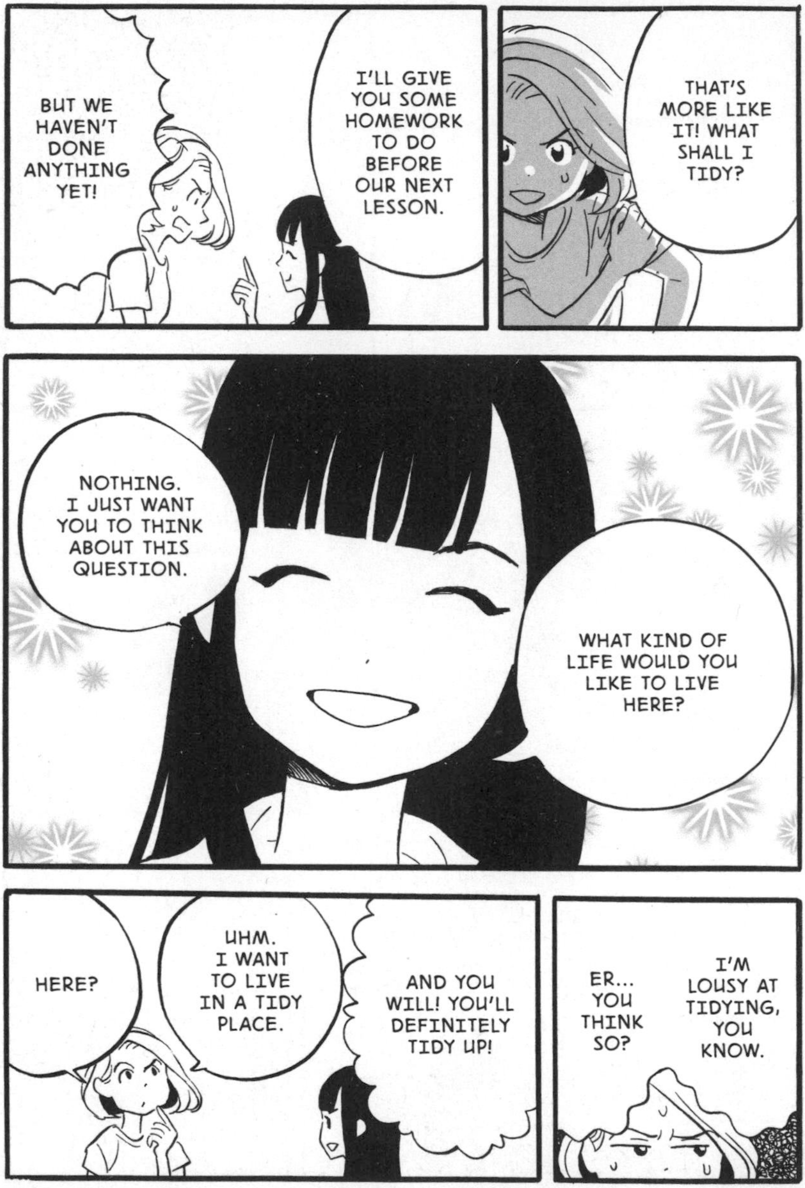
BUT WE HAVEN'T DONE ANYTHING YET!
I'LL GIVE YOU SOME HOMEWORK TO DO BEFORE OUR NEXT LESSON.
THAT'S MORE LIKE IT! WHAT SHALL I TIDY?
NOTHING. I JUST WANT YOU TO THINK ABOUT THIS QUESTION.
WHAT KIND OF LIFE WOULD YOU LIKE TO LIVE HERE?
HERE?
UHM. I WANT TO LIVE IN A TIDY PLACE.
AND YOU WILL! YOU'LL DEFINITELY TIDY UP!
I'M LOUSY AT TIDYING, YOU KNOW.
ER... YOU THINK SO?

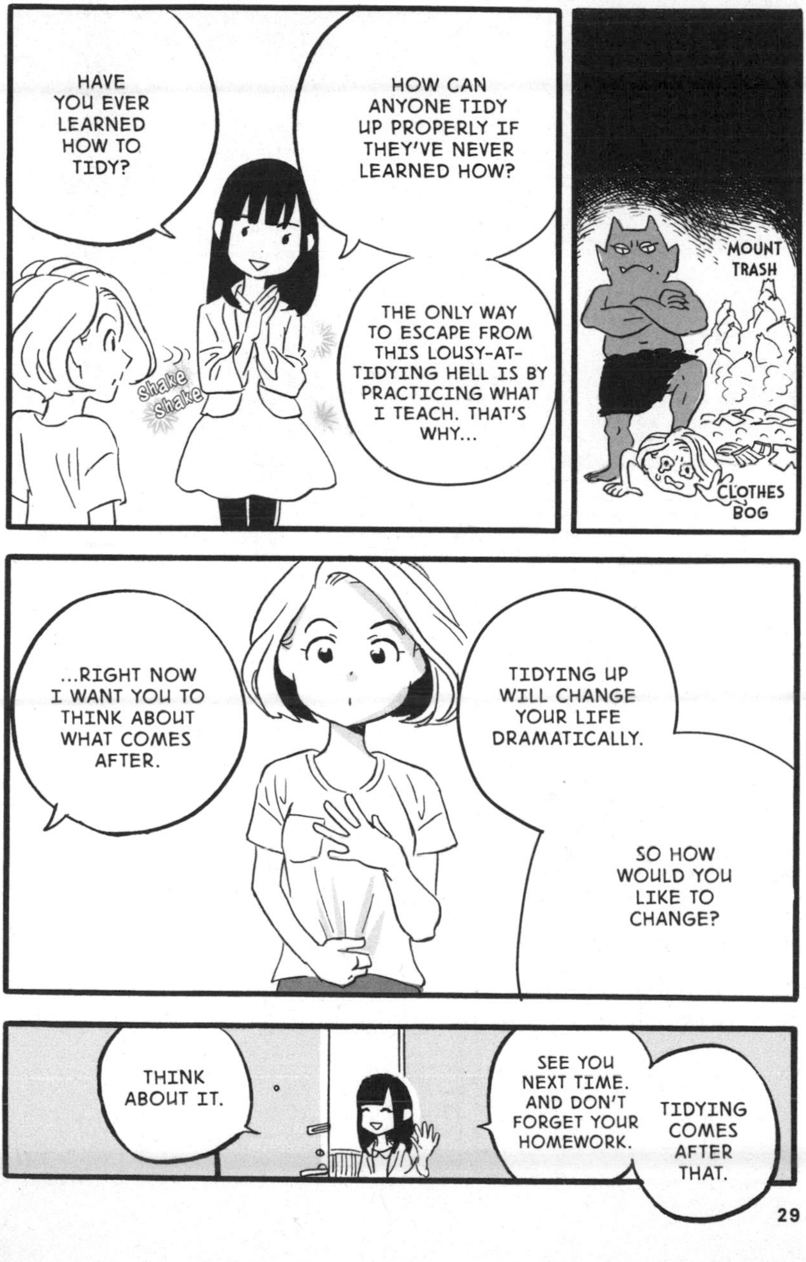
HAVE YOU EVER LEARNED HOW TO TIDY?
HOW CAN ANYONE TIDY UP PROPERLY IF THEY'VE NEVER LEARNED HOW?
Shake Shake
THE ONLY WAY TO ESCAPE FROM THIS LOUSY-AT-TIDYING HELL IS BY PRACTICING WHAT I TEACH. THAT'S WHY...
MOUNT TRASH
CLOTHES BOG
...RIGHT NOW I WANT YOU TO THINK ABOUT WHAT COMES AFTER.
TIDYING UP WILL CHANGE YOUR LIFE DRAMATICALLY.
SO HOW WOULD YOU LIKE TO CHANGE?
THINK ABOUT IT.
SEE YOU NEXT TIME. AND DON'T FORGET YOUR HOMEWORK.
TIDYING COMES AFTER THAT.

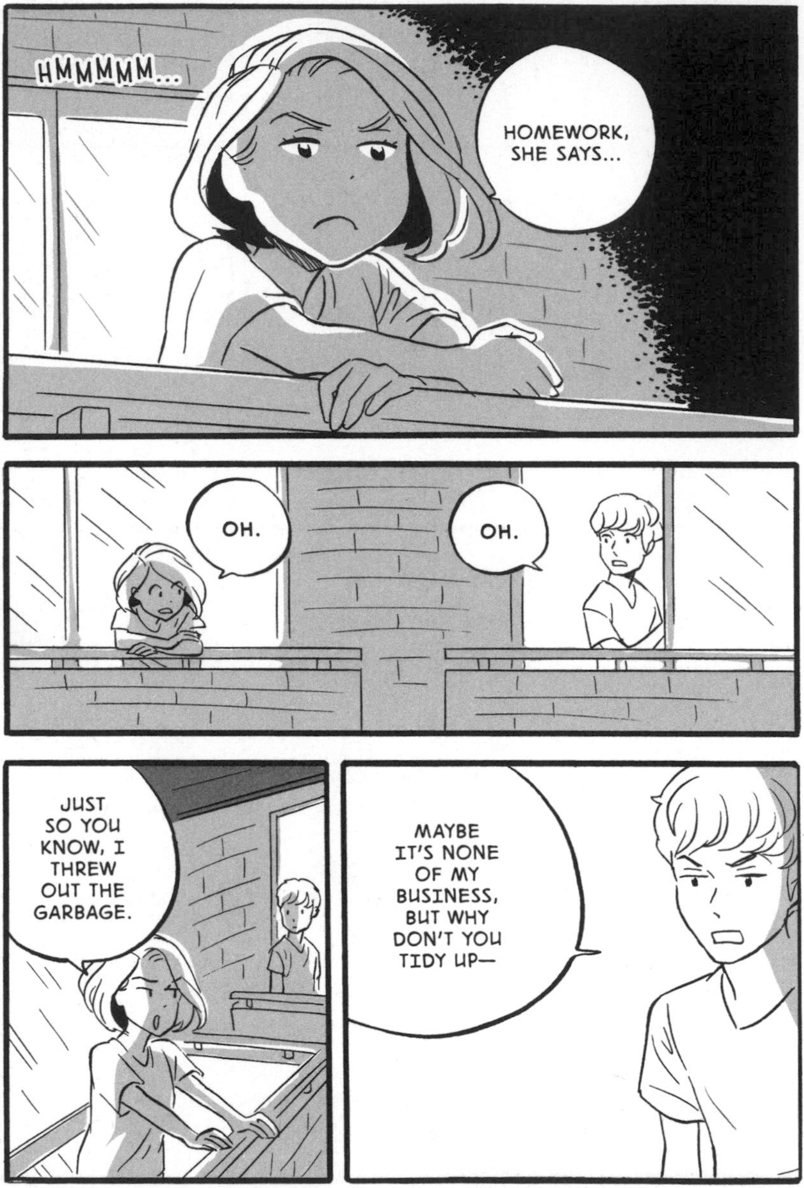
HMMMMM...
HOMEWORK, SHE SAYS...
OH.
OH.
JUST SO YOU KNOW, I THREW OUT THE GARBAGE.
MAYBE IT'S NONE OF MY BUSINESS, BUT WHY DON'T YOU TIDY UP—

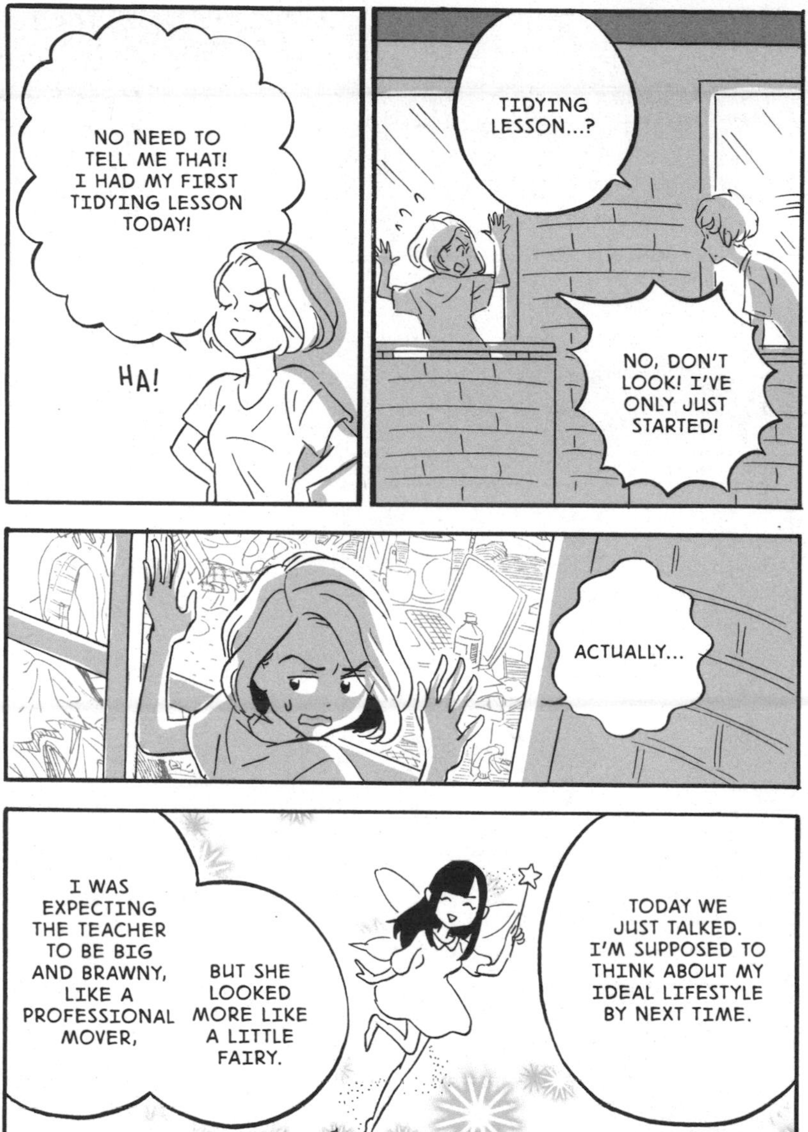
NO NEED TO TELL ME THAT! I HAD MY FIRST TIDYING LESSON TODAY!
HA!
TIDYING LESSON...?
NO, DON'T LOOK! I'VE ONLY JUST STARTED!
ACTUALLY...
I WAS EXPECTING THE TEACHER TO BE BIG AND BRAWNY, LIKE A PROFESSIONAL MOVER,
BUT SHE LOOKED MORE LIKE A LITTLE FAIRY.
TODAY WE JUST TALKED. I'M SUPPOSED TO THINK ABOUT MY IDEAL LIFESTYLE BY NEXT TIME.

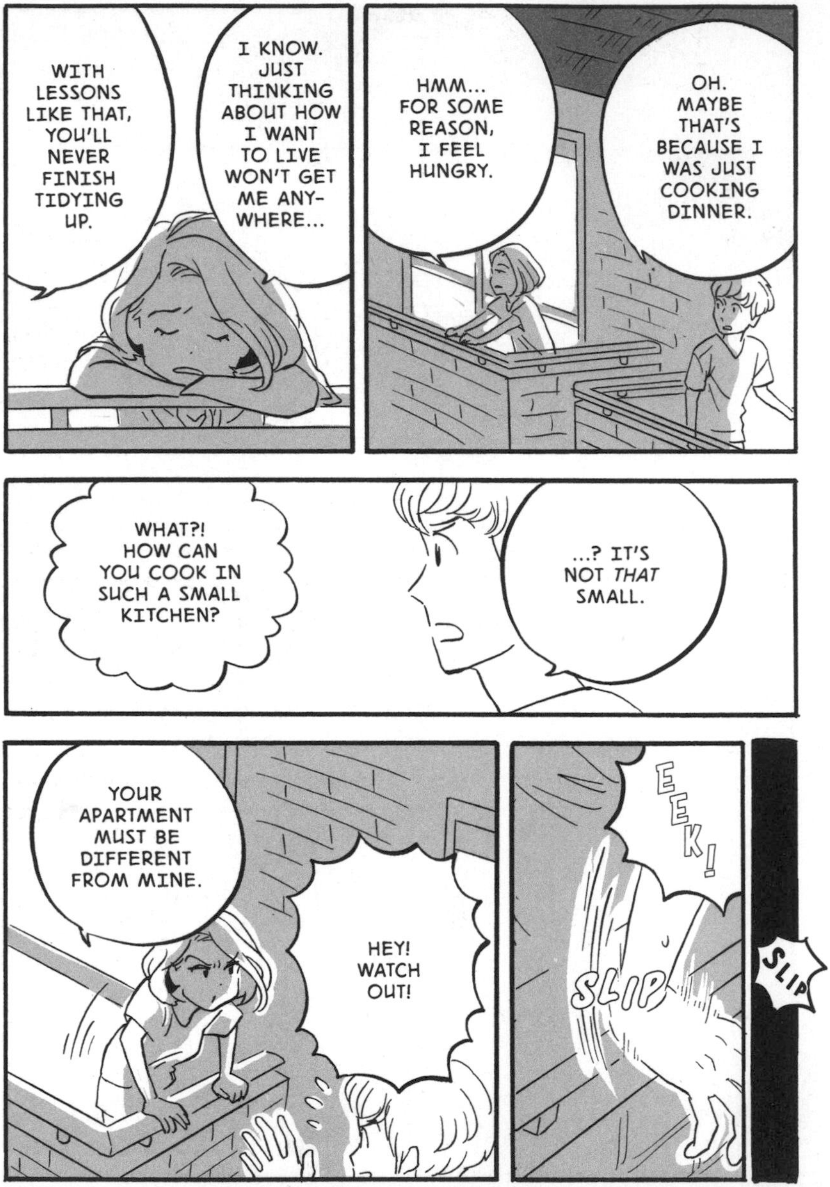
WITH LESSONS LIKE THAT, YOU'LL NEVER FINISH TIDYING UP.
I KNOW. JUST THINKING ABOUT HOW I WANT TO LIVE WON'T GET ME ANY-WHERE...
HMM... FOR SOME REASON, I FEEL HUNGRY.
OH. MAYBE THAT'S BECAUSE I WAS JUST COOKING DINNER.
WHAT?! HOW CAN YOU COOK IN SUCH A SMALL KITCHEN?
...? IT'S NOT *THAT* SMALL.
YOUR APARTMENT MUST BE DIFFERENT FROM MINE.
HEY! WATCH OUT!
EEK!
SLIP
SLIP

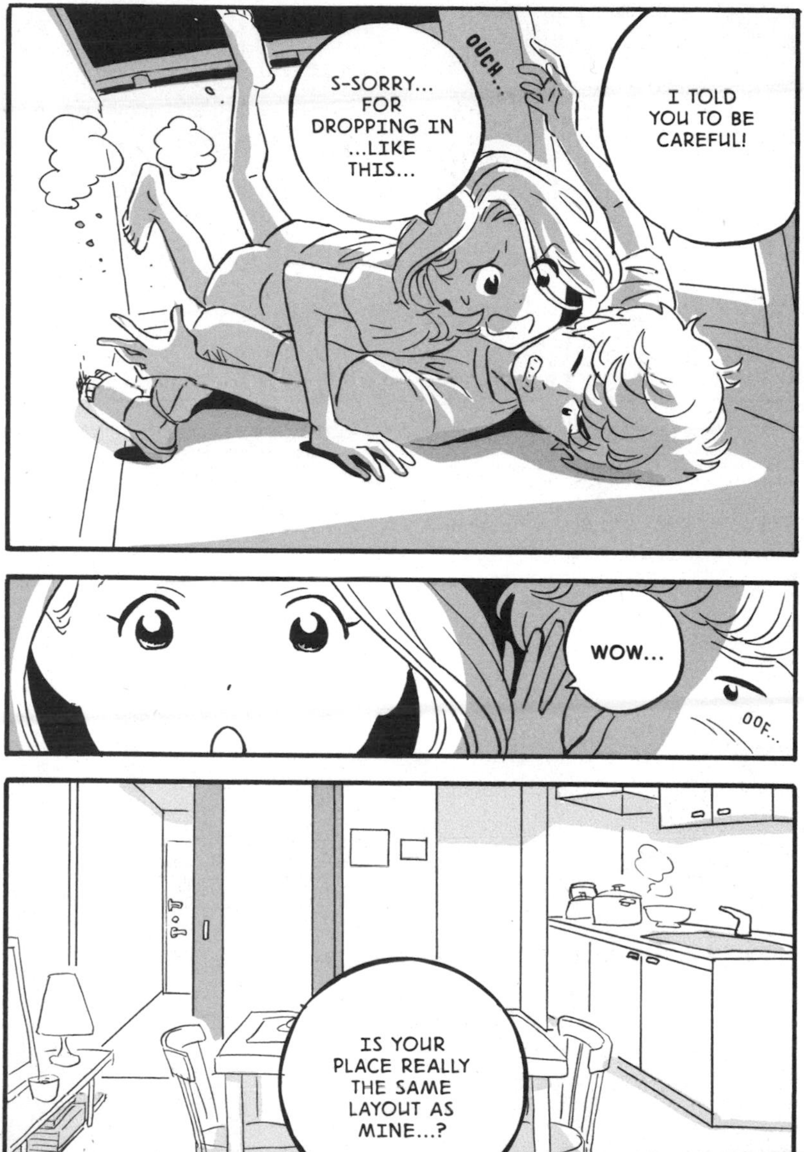
OUCH...
S-SORRY... FOR DROPPING IN ...LIKE THIS...
I TOLD YOU TO BE CAREFUL!
WOW...
OOF...
IS YOUR PLACE REALLY THE SAME LAYOUT AS MINE...?

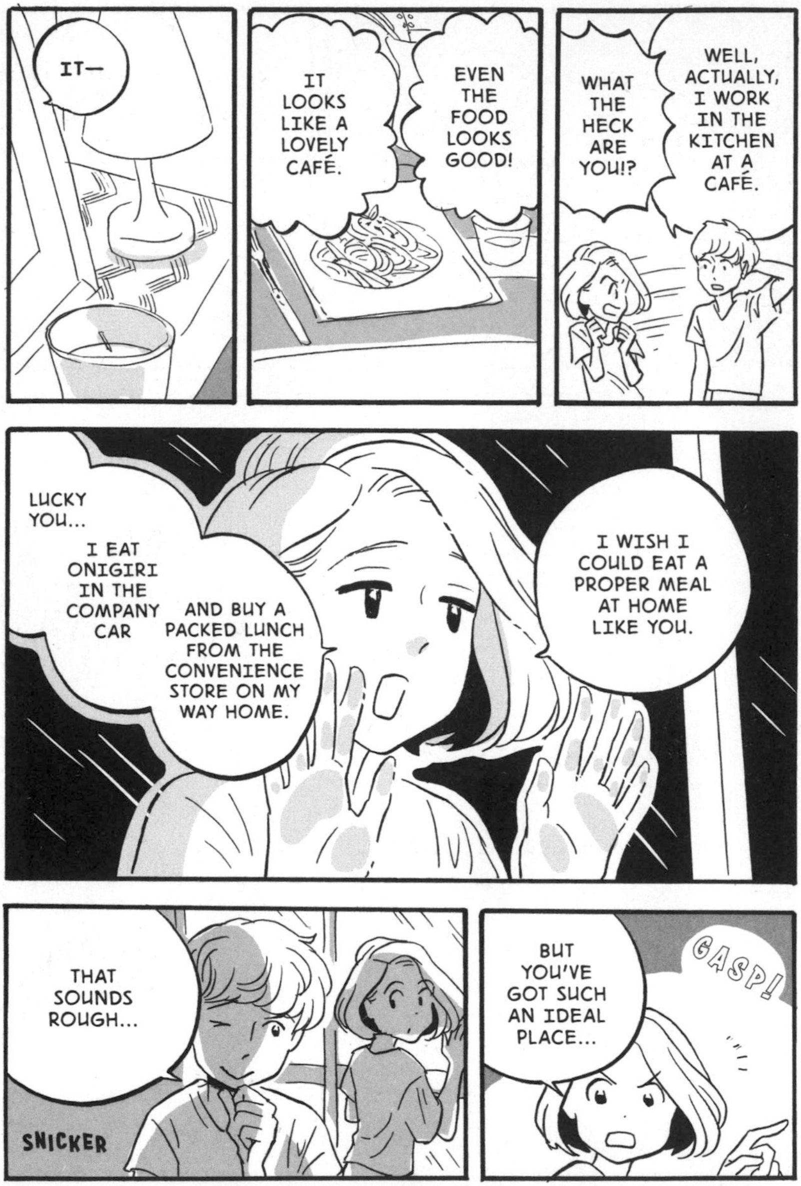
IT—
IT LOOKS LIKE A LOVELY CAFÉ.
EVEN THE FOOD LOOKS GOOD!
WHAT THE HECK ARE YOU!?
WELL, ACTUALLY, I WORK IN THE KITCHEN AT A CAFÉ.
LUCKY YOU...
I EAT ONIGIRI IN THE COMPANY CAR
AND BUY A PACKED LUNCH FROM THE CONVENIENCE STORE ON MY WAY HOME.
I WISH I COULD EAT A PROPER MEAL AT HOME LIKE YOU.
THAT SOUNDS ROUGH...
SNICKER
BUT YOU'VE GOT SUCH AN IDEAL PLACE...
GASP!

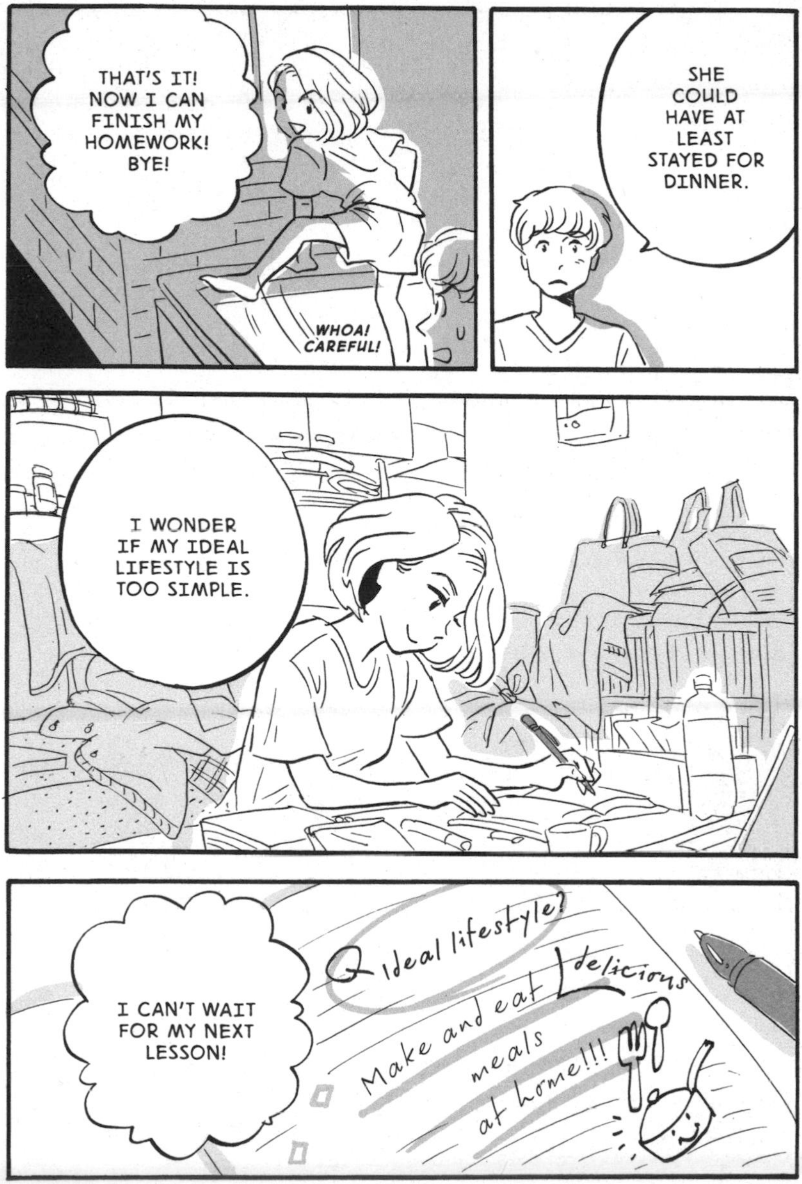
THAT'S IT! NOW I CAN FINISH MY HOMEWORK! BYE!
WHOA! CAREFUL!
SHE COULD HAVE AT LEAST STAYED FOR DINNER.
I WONDER IF MY IDEAL LIFESTYLE IS TOO SIMPLE.
I CAN'T WAIT FOR MY NEXT LESSON!
Q ideal lifestyle?
Make and eat delicious meals at home!!!

It all starts with visualizing your ideal lifestyle.

———

Start by thinking about how you really want to live. What kind of house would you like and what kind of life would you like to lead in it?

If you feel artistic, draw a picture. If you like writing, jot down your thoughts on paper. I also recommend cutting out photos of homes you like from interior decorating magazines.

By thinking about your ideal lifestyle, you will begin identifying why you really want to tidy and the kind of life you want once you have finished. That is how life-changing tidying can be.

finish
discarding
first

3

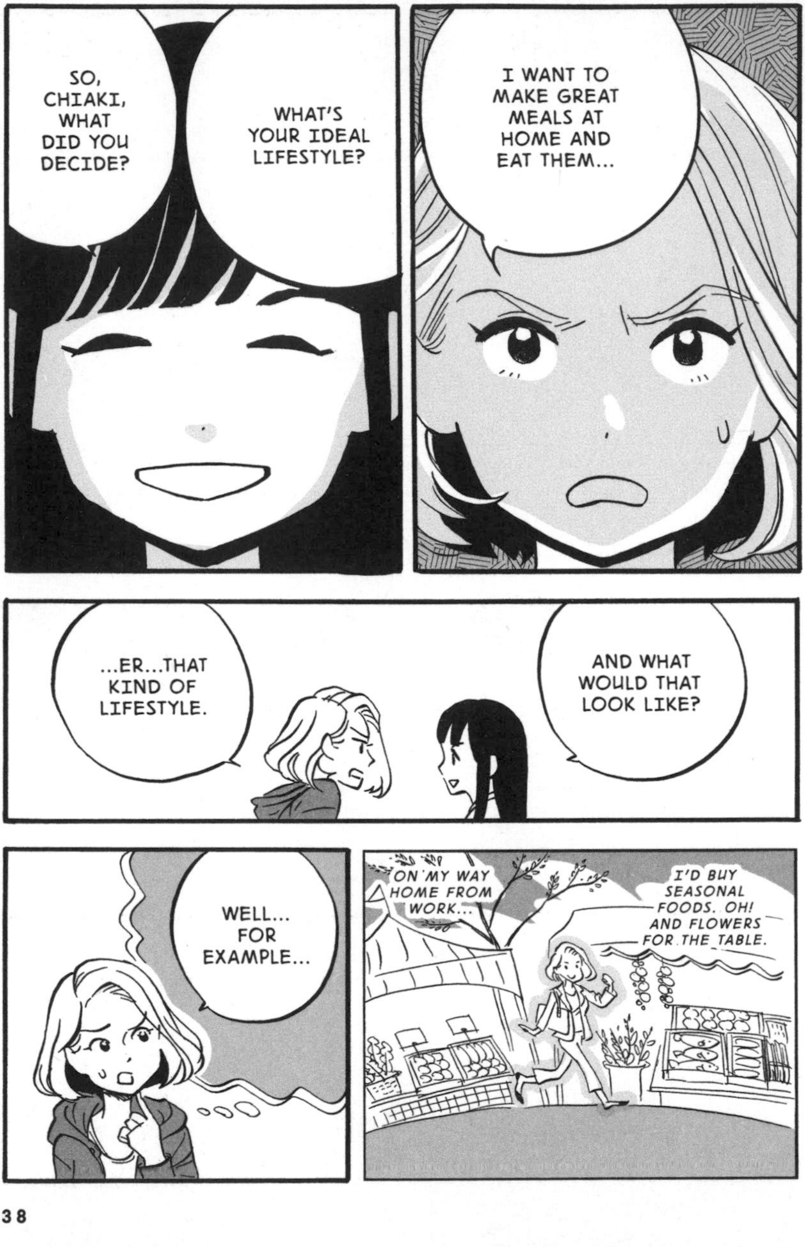
SO, CHIAKI, WHAT DID YOU DECIDE?
WHAT'S YOUR IDEAL LIFESTYLE?
I WANT TO MAKE GREAT MEALS AT HOME AND EAT THEM...
...ER...THAT KIND OF LIFESTYLE.
AND WHAT WOULD THAT LOOK LIKE?
WELL... FOR EXAMPLE...
ON MY WAY HOME FROM WORK...
I'D BUY SEASONAL FOODS. OH! AND FLOWERS FOR THE TABLE.

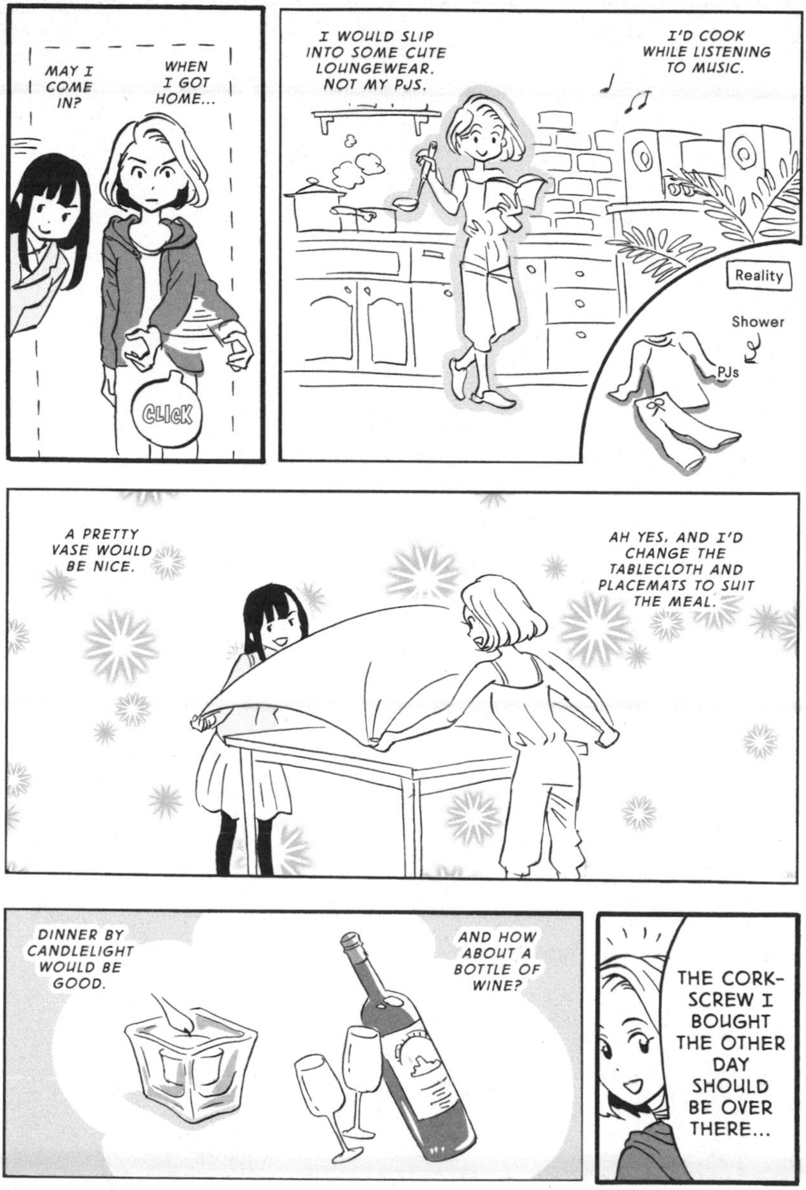

MAY I COME IN?
WHEN I GOT HOME...
CLICK
I WOULD SLIP INTO SOME CUTE LOUNGEWEAR. NOT MY PJS.
I'D COOK WHILE LISTENING TO MUSIC.
Reality
Shower
PJs
A PRETTY VASE WOULD BE NICE.
AH YES, AND I'D CHANGE THE TABLECLOTH AND PLACEMATS TO SUIT THE MEAL.
DINNER BY CANDLELIGHT WOULD BE GOOD.
AND HOW ABOUT A BOTTLE OF WINE?
THE CORK-SCREW I BOUGHT THE OTHER DAY SHOULD BE OVER THERE...

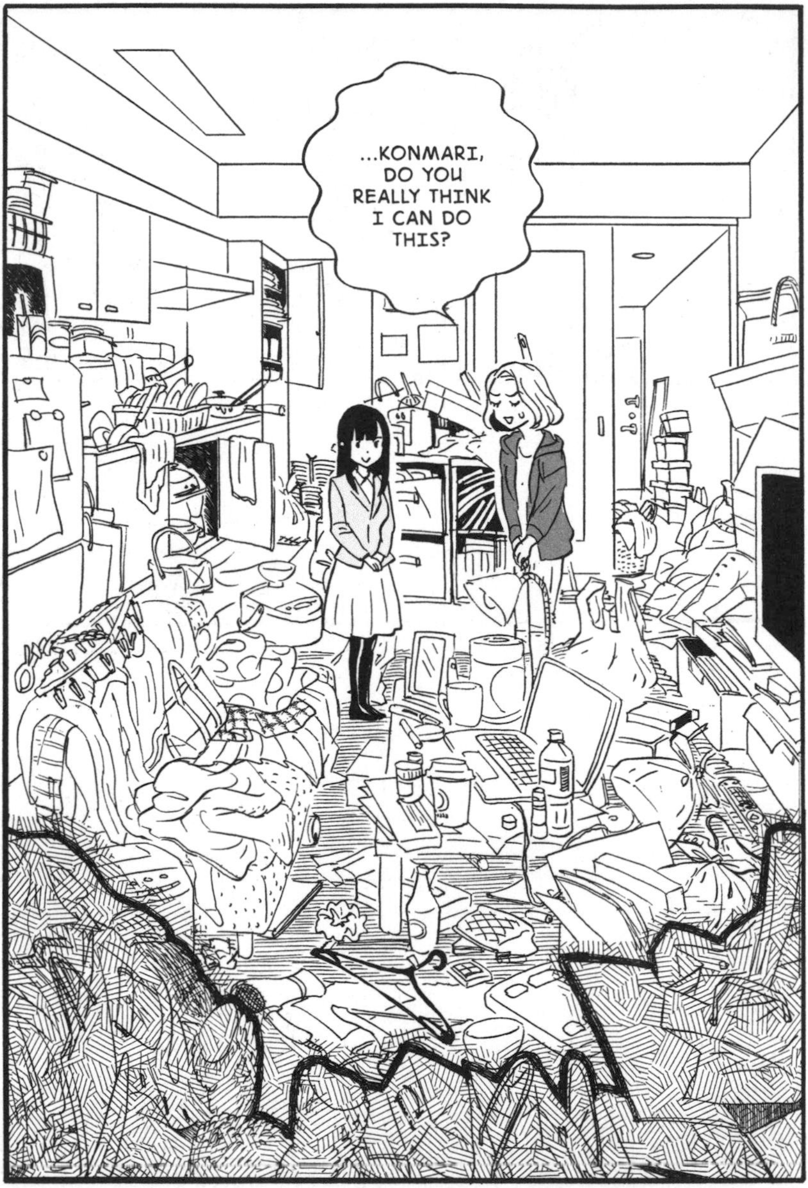
...KONMARI, DO YOU REALLY THINK I CAN DO THIS?

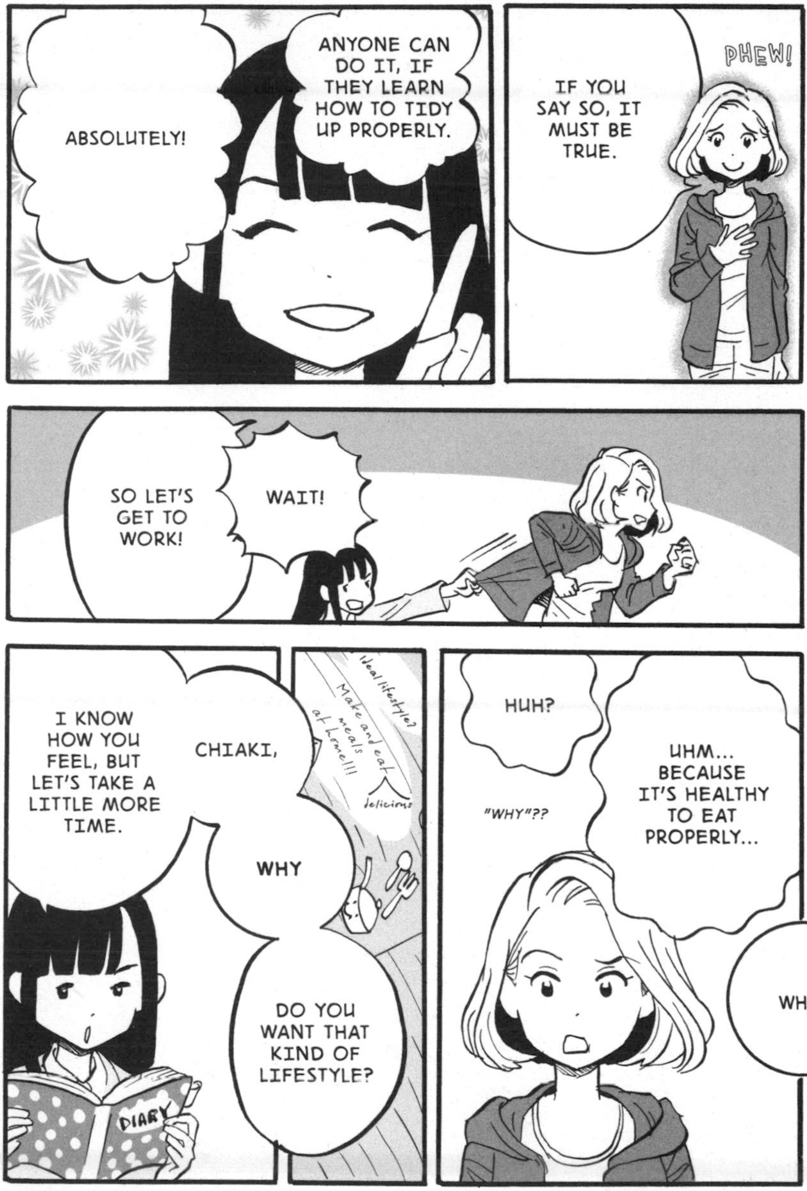
ABSOLUTELY!
ANYONE CAN DO IT, IF THEY LEARN HOW TO TIDY UP PROPERLY.
IF YOU SAY SO, IT MUST BE TRUE.
PHEW!
SO LET'S GET TO WORK!
WAIT!
I KNOW HOW YOU FEEL, BUT LET'S TAKE A LITTLE MORE TIME.
CHIAKI,
WHY
DO YOU WANT THAT KIND OF LIFESTYLE?
DIARY
Ideal lifestyle?
Make and eat meals at home!!!
delicious
HUH?
"WHY"??
UHM... BECAUSE IT'S HEALTHY TO EAT PROPERLY...
WHY?

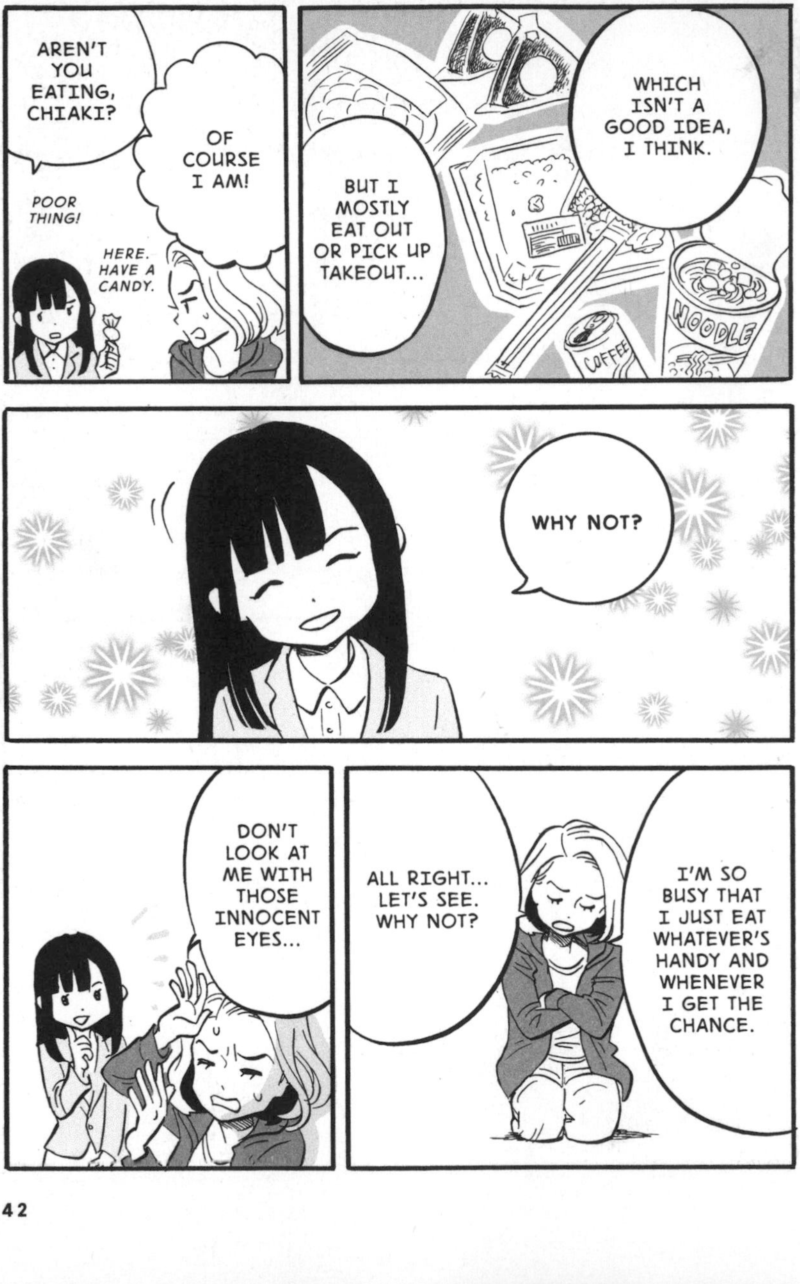
AREN'T YOU EATING, CHIAKI?
OF COURSE I AM!
POOR THING!
HERE. HAVE A CANDY.
BUT I MOSTLY EAT OUT OR PICK UP TAKEOUT...
WHICH ISN'T A GOOD IDEA, I THINK.
NOODLE
COFFEE
WHY NOT?
DON'T LOOK AT ME WITH THOSE INNOCENT EYES...
ALL RIGHT... LET'S SEE. WHY NOT?
I'M SO BUSY THAT I JUST EAT WHATEVER'S HANDY AND WHENEVER I GET THE CHANCE.

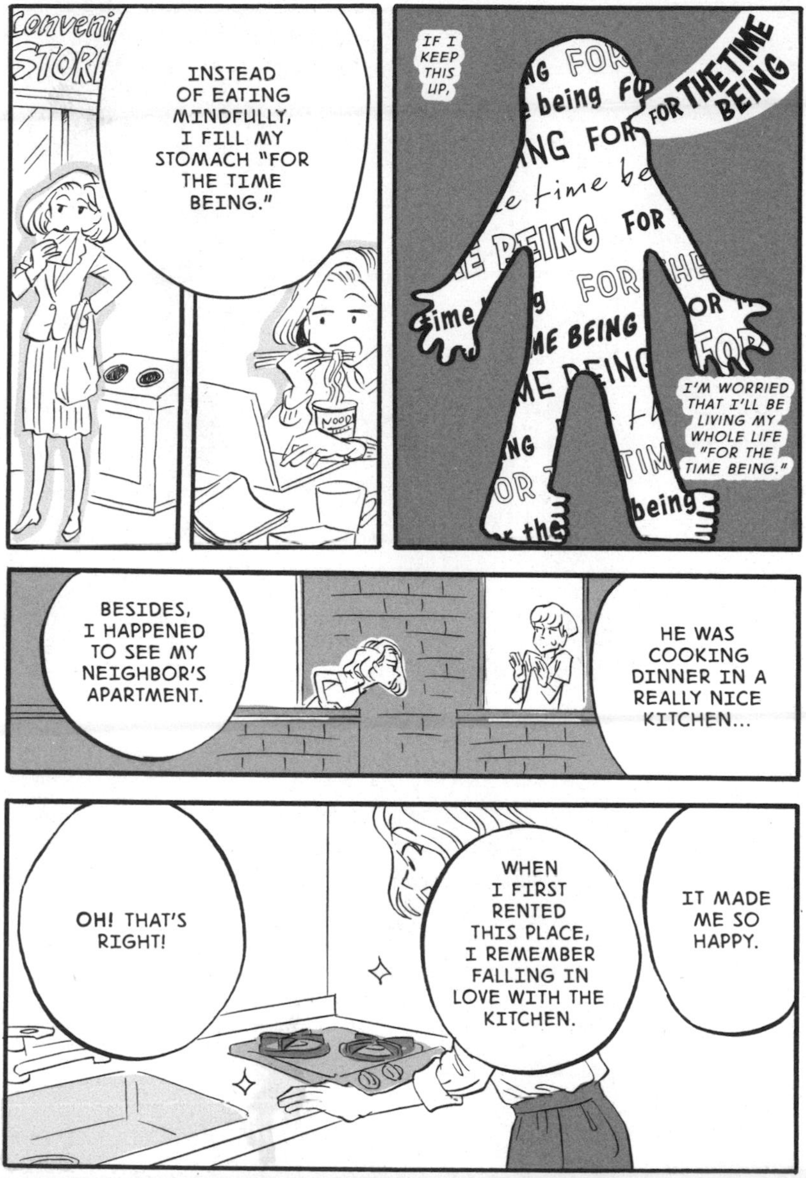
Conveni
STORE
INSTEAD OF EATING MINDFULLY, I FILL MY STOMACH "FOR THE TIME BEING."
IF I KEEP THIS UP,
FOR THE TIME BEING
I'M WORRIED THAT I'LL BE LIVING MY WHOLE LIFE "FOR THE TIME BEING."
BESIDES, I HAPPENED TO SEE MY NEIGHBOR'S APARTMENT.
HE WAS COOKING DINNER IN A REALLY NICE KITCHEN...
OH! THAT'S RIGHT!
WHEN I FIRST RENTED THIS PLACE, I REMEMBER FALLING IN LOVE WITH THE KITCHEN.
IT MADE ME SO HAPPY.

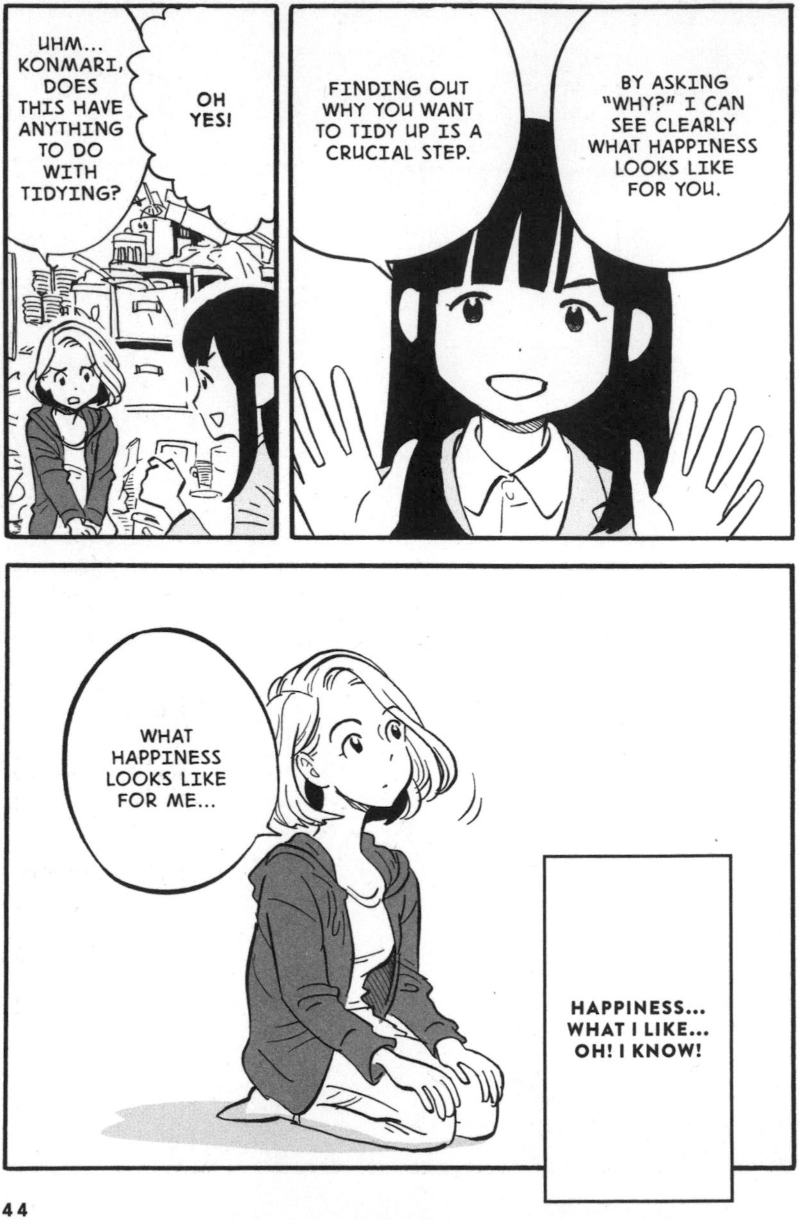
UHM... KONMARI, DOES THIS HAVE ANYTHING TO DO WITH TIDYING?
OH YES!
FINDING OUT WHY YOU WANT TO TIDY UP IS A CRUCIAL STEP.
BY ASKING "WHY?" I CAN SEE CLEARLY WHAT HAPPINESS LOOKS LIKE FOR YOU.
WHAT HAPPINESS LOOKS LIKE FOR ME...
HAPPINESS... WHAT I LIKE... OH! I KNOW!

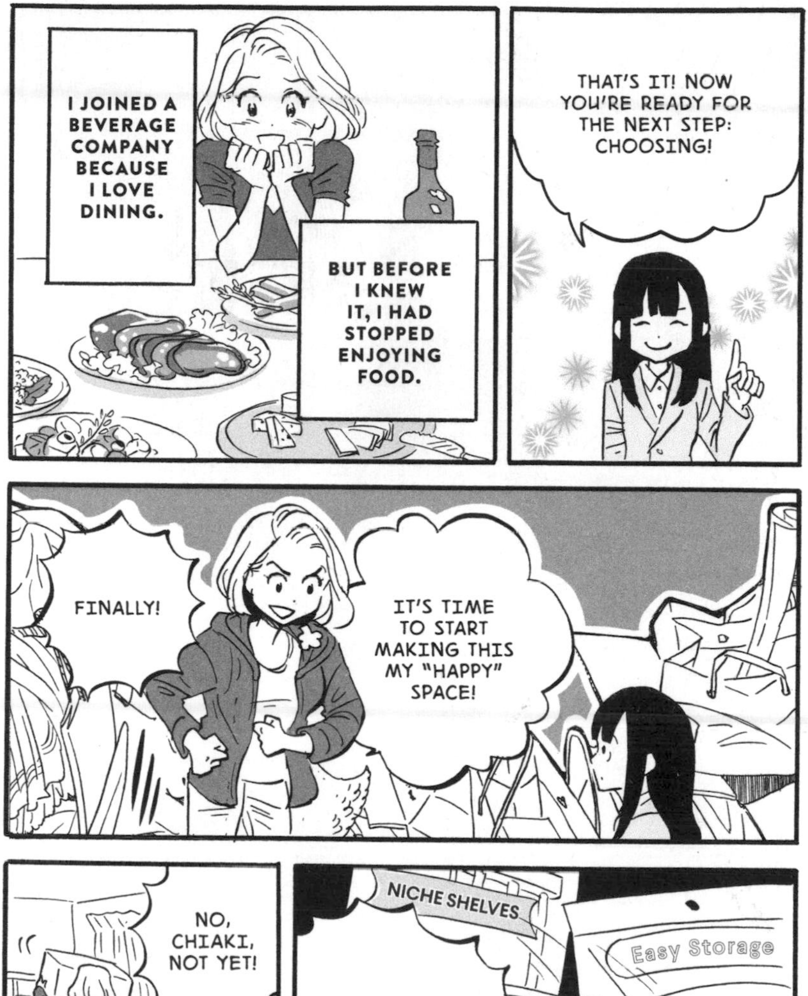
I JOINED A BEVERAGE COMPANY BECAUSE I LOVE DINING.
BUT BEFORE I KNEW IT, I HAD STOPPED ENJOYING FOOD.
THAT'S IT! NOW YOU'RE READY FOR THE NEXT STEP: CHOOSING!
FINALLY!
IT'S TIME TO START MAKING THIS MY "HAPPY" SPACE!
NO, CHIAKI, NOT YET!
NICHE SHELVES
Easy Storage
LOOK! I'M PREPARED! TAKE YOUR PICK!
STORAGE BOX
Set of 3

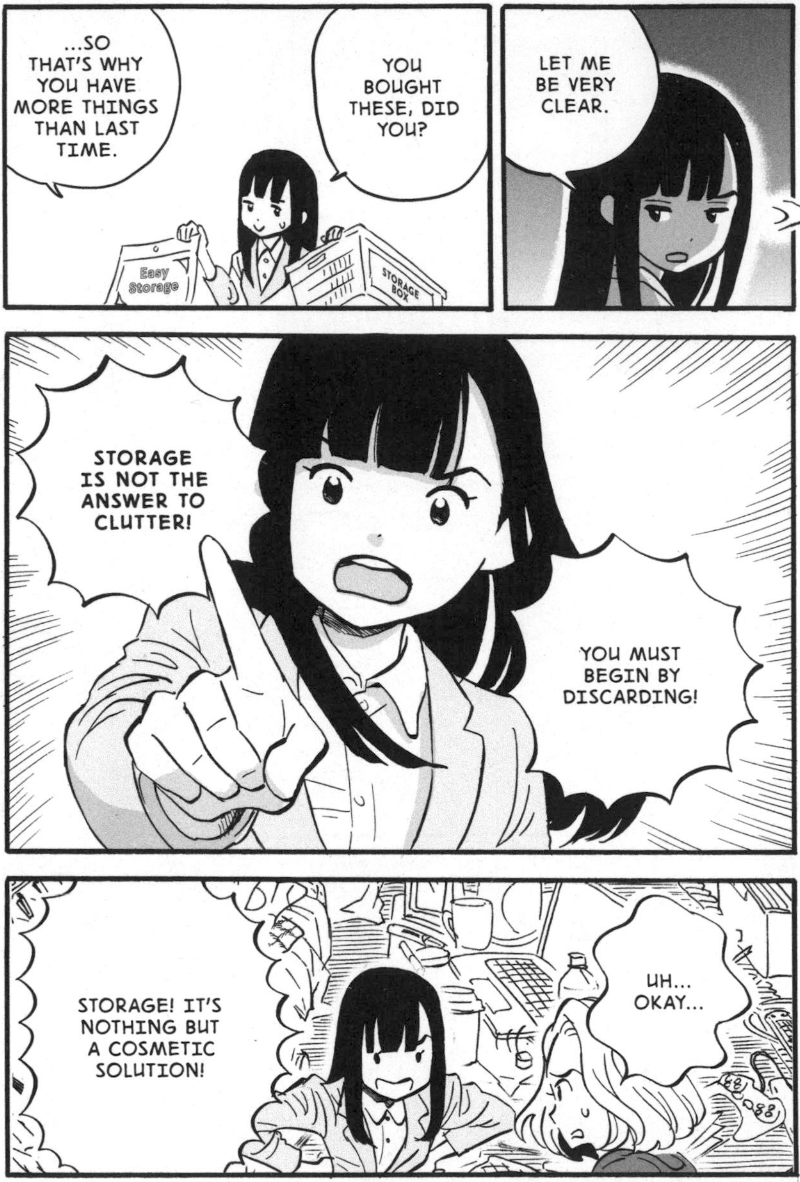
...SO THAT'S WHY YOU HAVE MORE THINGS THAN LAST TIME.
YOU BOUGHT THESE, DID YOU?
Easy Storage
STORAGE BOX
LET ME BE VERY CLEAR.
STORAGE IS NOT THE ANSWER TO CLUTTER!
YOU MUST BEGIN BY DISCARDING!
STORAGE! IT'S NOTHING BUT A COSMETIC SOLUTION!
UH... OKAY...

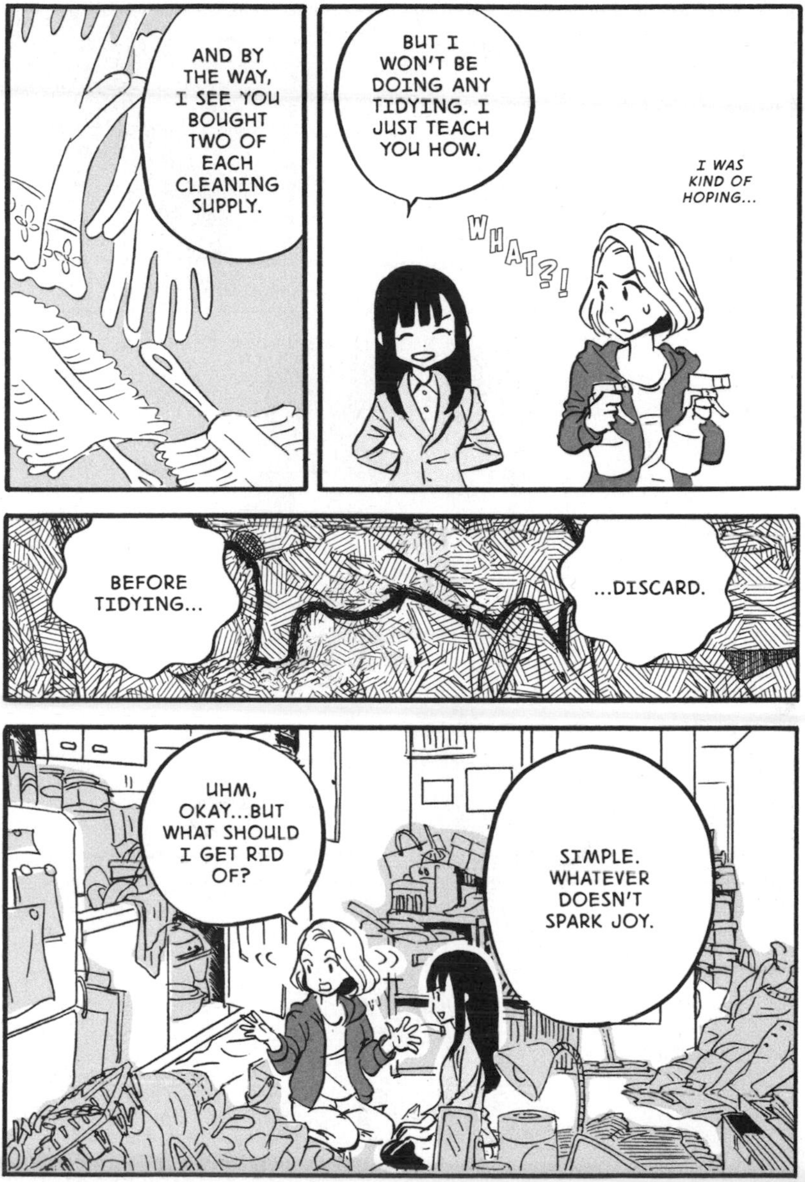
AND BY THE WAY, I SEE YOU BOUGHT TWO OF EACH CLEANING SUPPLY.
BUT I WON'T BE DOING ANY TIDYING. I JUST TEACH YOU HOW.
I WAS KIND OF HOPING...
WHAT?!
BEFORE TIDYING...
...DISCARD.
UHM, OKAY...BUT WHAT SHOULD I GET RID OF?
SIMPLE. WHATEVER DOESN'T SPARK JOY.

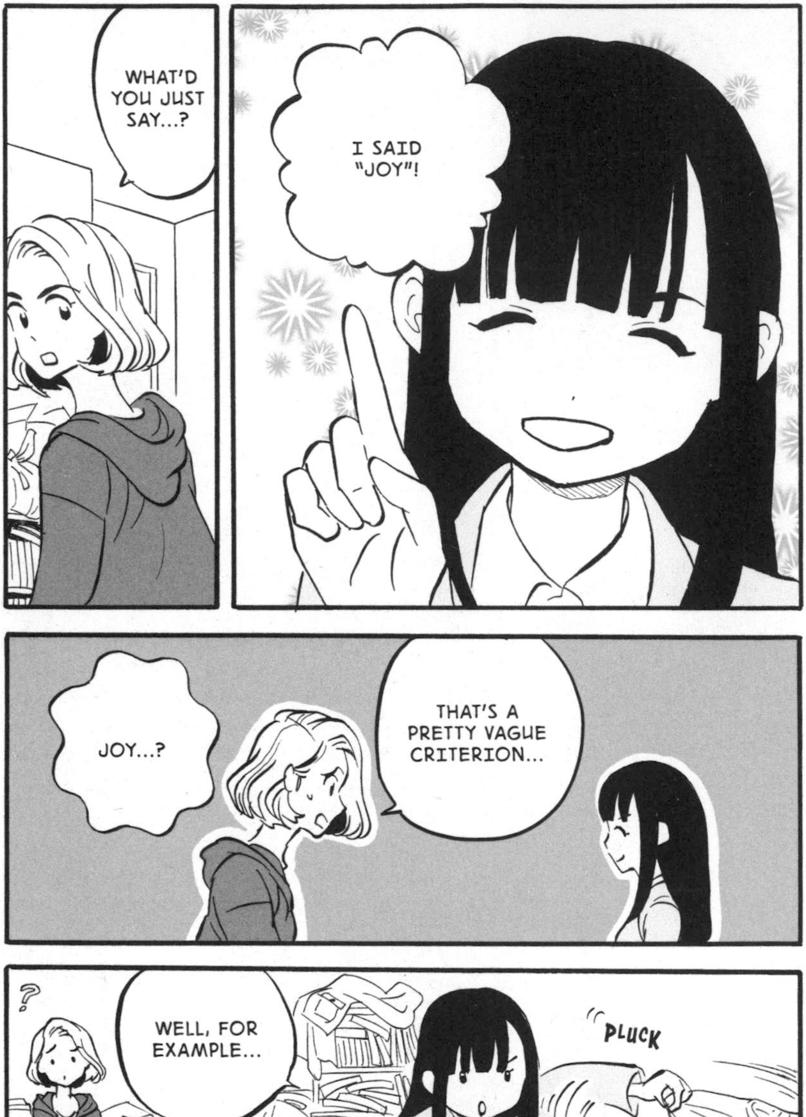
WHAT'D YOU JUST SAY...?
I SAID "JOY"!
JOY...?
THAT'S A PRETTY VAGUE CRITERION...
?
WELL, FOR EXAMPLE...
PLUCK
PLUCK

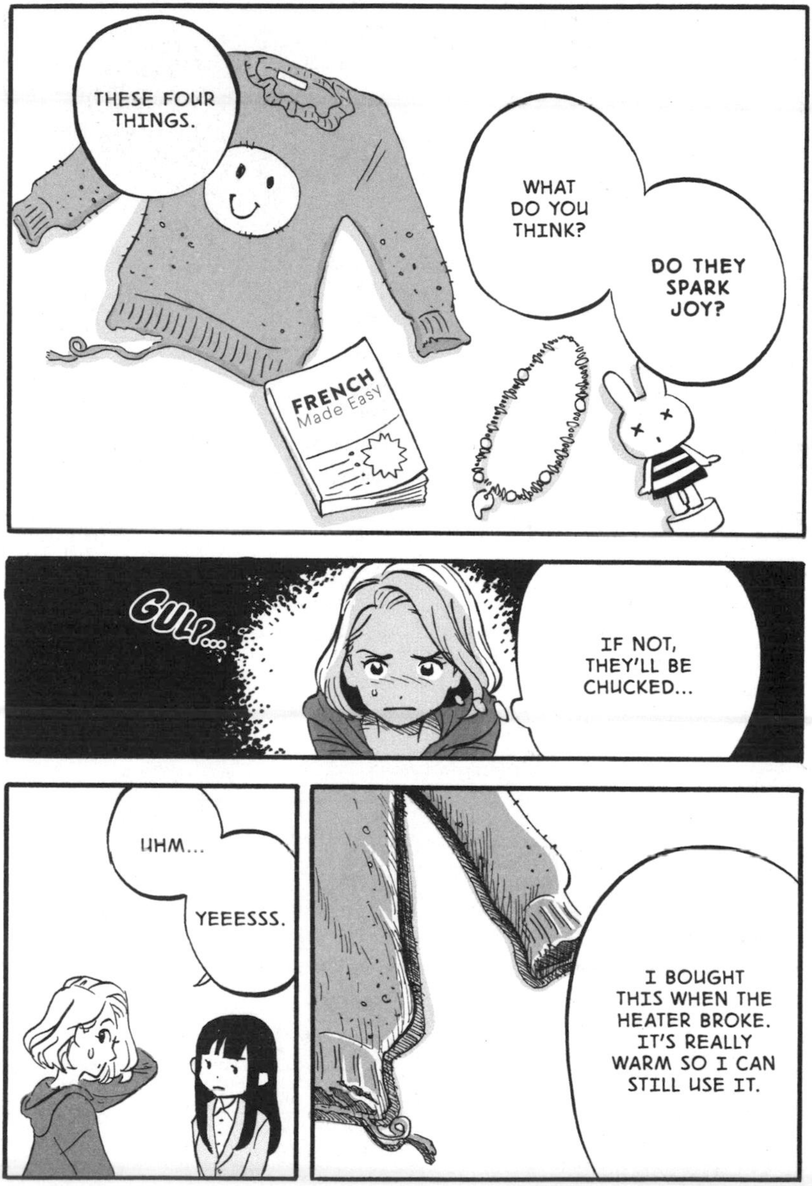

THESE FOUR THINGS.
WHAT DO YOU THINK?
DO THEY SPARK JOY?
FRENCH Made Easy
GULP...
IF NOT, THEY'LL BE CHUCKED...
UHM...
YEEESSS.
I BOUGHT THIS WHEN THE HEATER BROKE. IT'S REALLY WARM SO I CAN STILL USE IT.

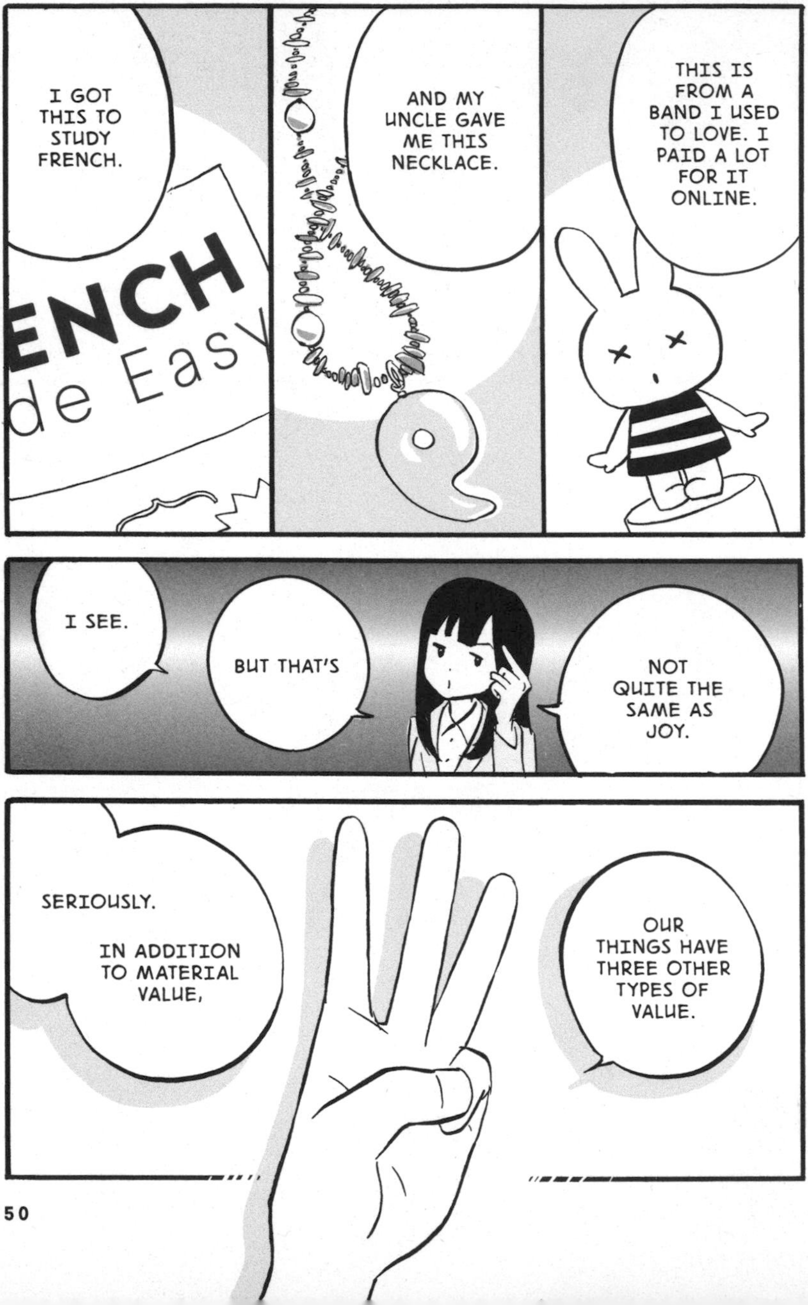
I GOT THIS TO STUDY FRENCH.
ENCH
de Easy
AND MY UNCLE GAVE ME THIS NECKLACE.
THIS IS FROM A BAND I USED TO LOVE. I PAID A LOT FOR IT ONLINE.
I SEE.
BUT THAT'S
NOT QUITE THE SAME AS JOY.
SERIOUSLY.
IN ADDITION TO MATERIAL VALUE,
OUR THINGS HAVE THREE OTHER TYPES OF VALUE.

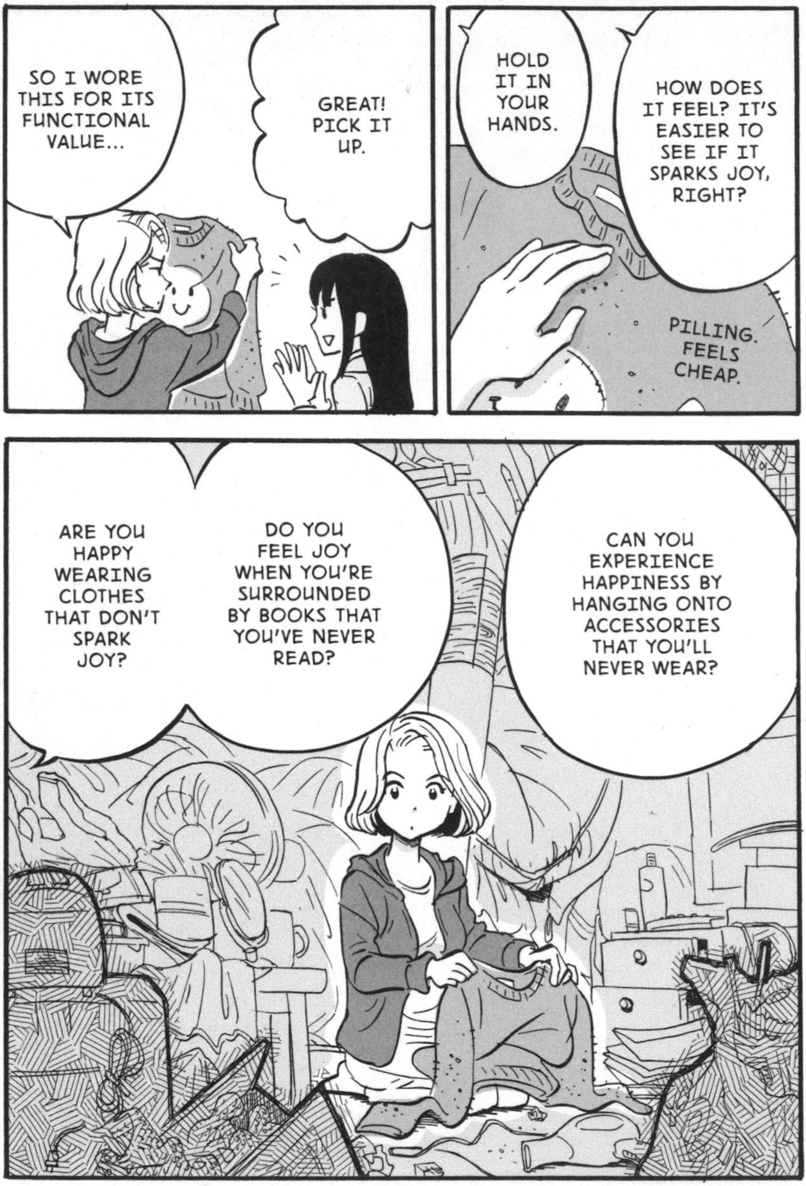
SO I WORE THIS FOR ITS FUNCTIONAL VALUE...
GREAT! PICK IT UP.
HOLD IT IN YOUR HANDS.
HOW DOES IT FEEL? IT'S EASIER TO SEE IF IT SPARKS JOY, RIGHT?
PILLING. FEELS CHEAP.
ARE YOU HAPPY WEARING CLOTHES THAT DON'T SPARK JOY?
DO YOU FEEL JOY WHEN YOU'RE SURROUNDED BY BOOKS THAT YOU'VE NEVER READ?
CAN YOU EXPERIENCE HAPPINESS BY HANGING ONTO ACCESSORIES THAT YOU'LL NEVER WEAR?

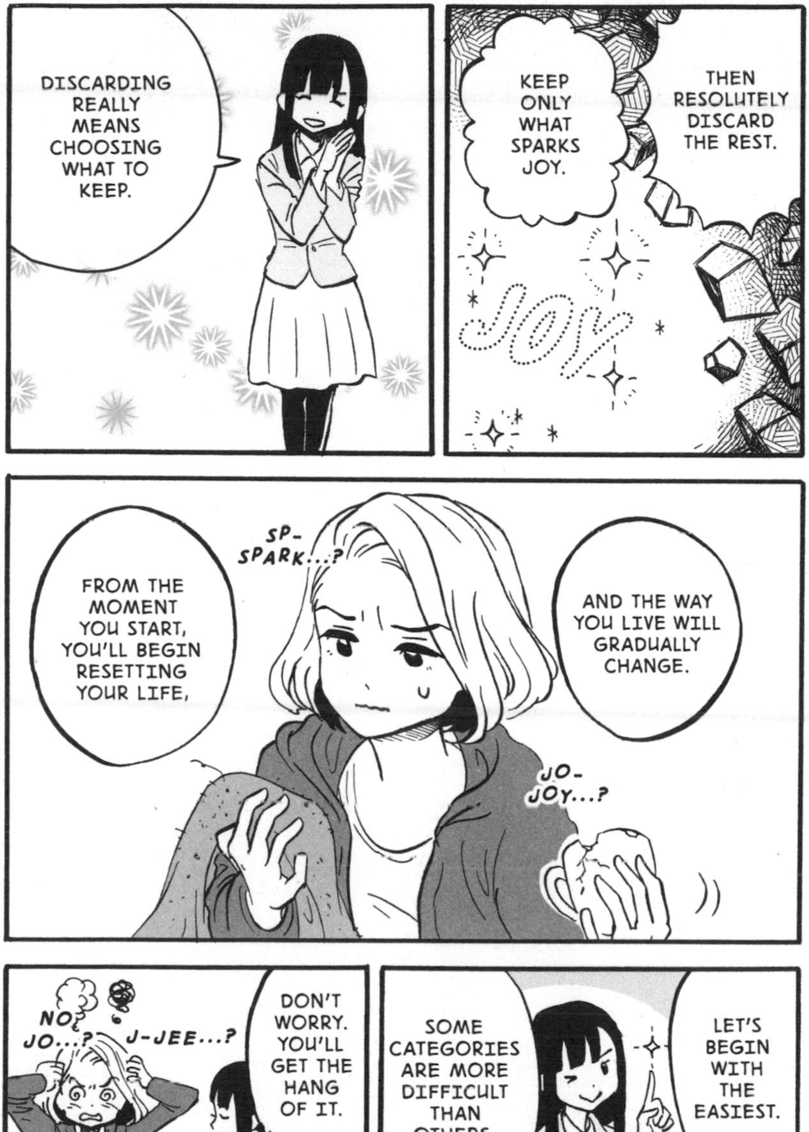
DISCARDING REALLY MEANS CHOOSING WHAT TO KEEP.
KEEP ONLY WHAT SPARKS JOY.
THEN RESOLUTELY DISCARD THE REST.
JOY
FROM THE MOMENT YOU START, YOU'LL BEGIN RESETTING YOUR LIFE,
SP- SPARK...?
AND THE WAY YOU LIVE WILL GRADUALLY CHANGE.
JO- JOY...?
NO JO...?
J-JEE...?
DON'T WORRY. YOU'LL GET THE HANG OF IT.
EEHEEHEE
SOME CATEGORIES ARE MORE DIFFICULT THAN OTHERS.
LET'S BEGIN WITH THE EASIEST.

Finish discarding first. But don't choose what to discard. Choose what to keep.

———

If you focus on what to throw away, you will lose sight of the real purpose of tidying.

The best criterion for choosing what to keep is this: Does it spark joy when you touch it?

Take each item in your hand. Keep those that spark joy and discard those that don't. This is the simplest and most accurate way to figure out what you should keep.

The true purpose of your home and your things is to bring you happiness. So, naturally, the criterion for choosing should be whether keeping something will make you happy—whether it will bring you joy.

4

tidy by
category

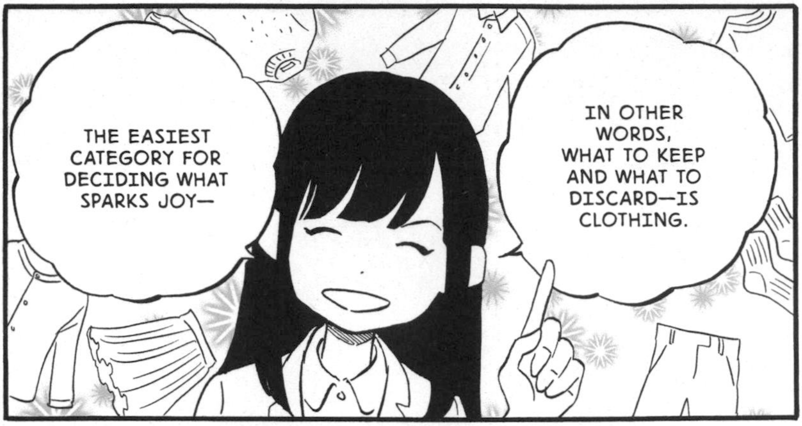
THE EASIEST CATEGORY FOR DECIDING WHAT SPARKS JOY—
IN OTHER WORDS, WHAT TO KEEP AND WHAT TO DISCARD—IS CLOTHING.

CLOTHING IS EASIEST BECAUSE IT'S A CLEARLY DEFINED CATEGORY WITHOUT MUCH "RARITY."

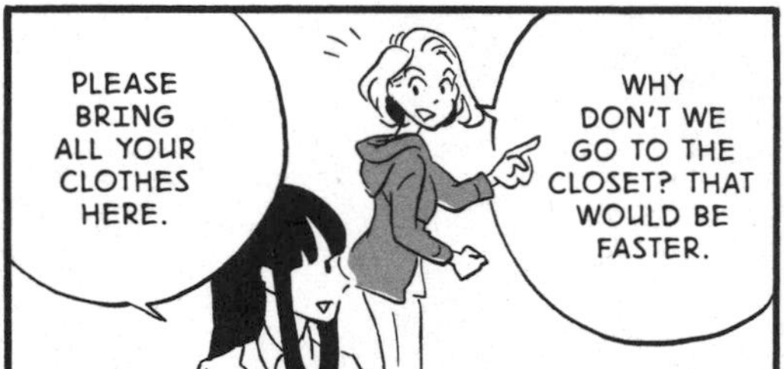
PLEASE BRING ALL YOUR CLOTHES HERE.
WHY DON'T WE GO TO THE CLOSET? THAT WOULD BE FASTER.

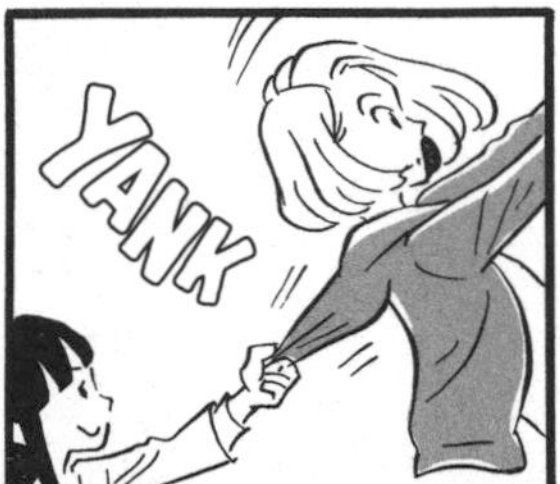
YANK

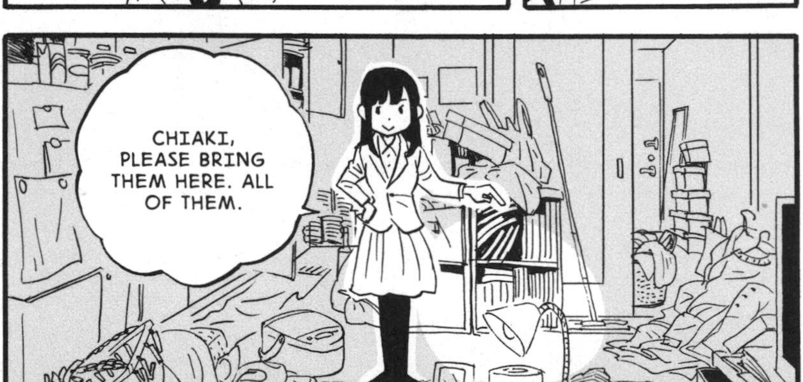
CHIAKI, PLEASE BRING THEM HERE. ALL OF THEM.

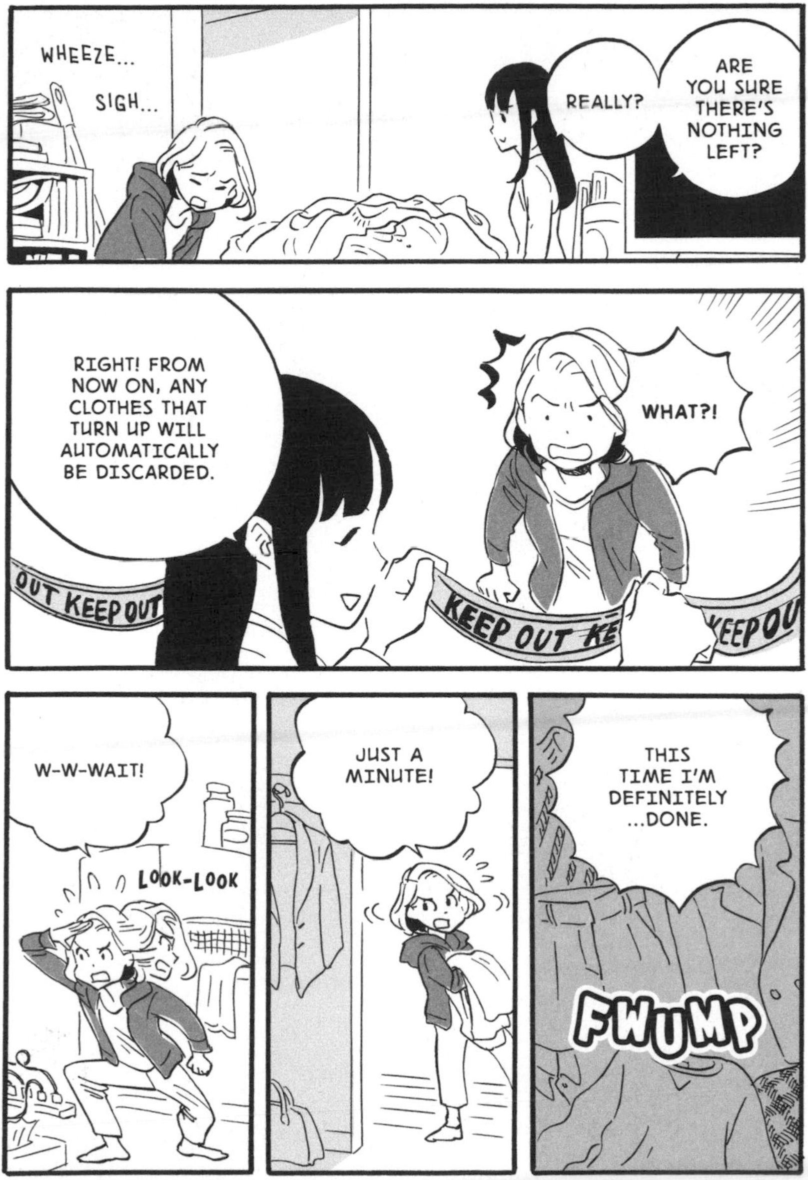
WHEEZE...
SIGH...
REALLY?
ARE YOU SURE THERE'S NOTHING LEFT?
RIGHT! FROM NOW ON, ANY CLOTHES THAT TURN UP WILL AUTOMATICALLY BE DISCARDED.
OUT KEEP OUT
KEEP OUT KE
KEEP OU
WHAT?!
W-W-WAIT!
LOOK-LOOK
JUST A MINUTE!
THIS TIME I'M DEFINITELY ...DONE.
FWUMP

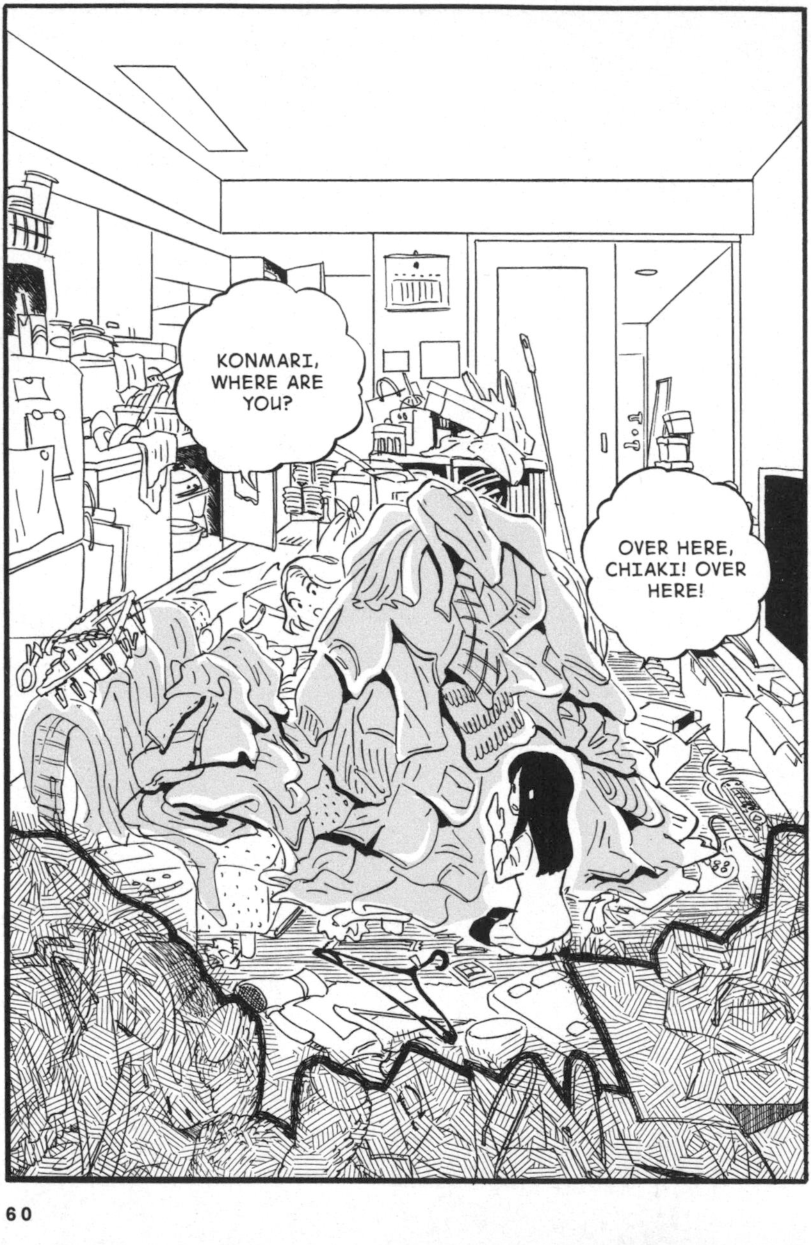
KONMARI, WHERE ARE YOU?
OVER HERE, CHIAKI! OVER HERE!

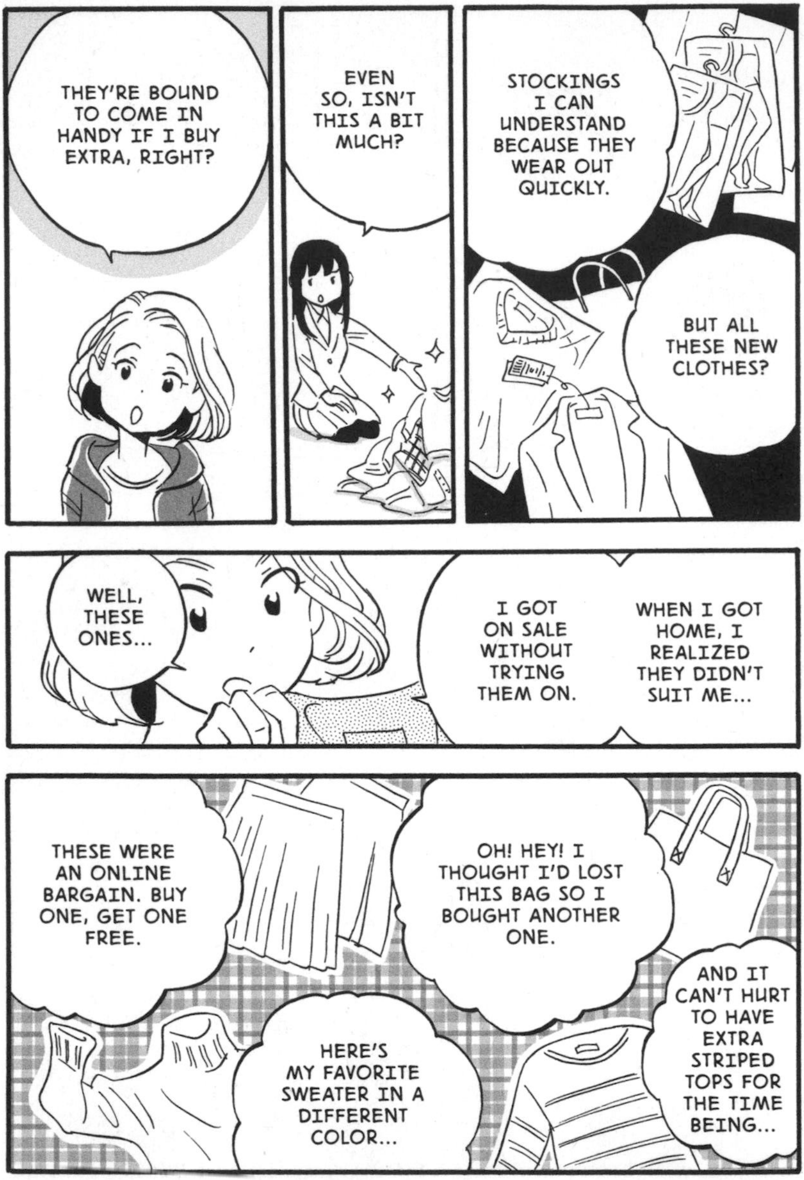
THEY'RE BOUND TO COME IN HANDY IF I BUY EXTRA, RIGHT?
EVEN SO, ISN'T THIS A BIT MUCH?
STOCKINGS I CAN UNDERSTAND BECAUSE THEY WEAR OUT QUICKLY.
BUT ALL THESE NEW CLOTHES?
WELL, THESE ONES...
I GOT ON SALE WITHOUT TRYING THEM ON.
WHEN I GOT HOME, I REALIZED THEY DIDN'T SUIT ME...
THESE WERE AN ONLINE BARGAIN. BUY ONE, GET ONE FREE.
OH! HEY! I THOUGHT I'D LOST THIS BAG SO I BOUGHT ANOTHER ONE.
HERE'S MY FAVORITE SWEATER IN A DIFFERENT COLOR...
AND IT CAN'T HURT TO HAVE EXTRA STRIPED TOPS FOR THE TIME BEING...

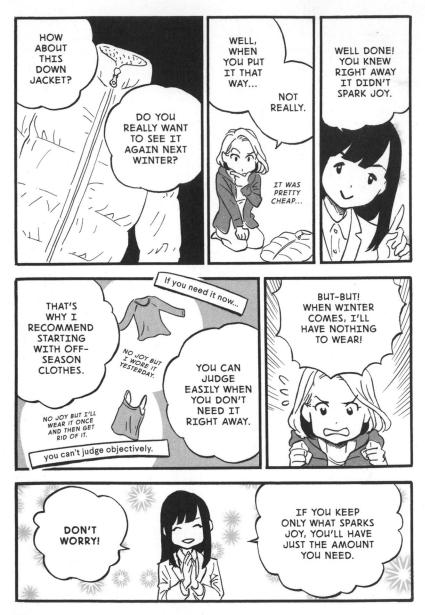

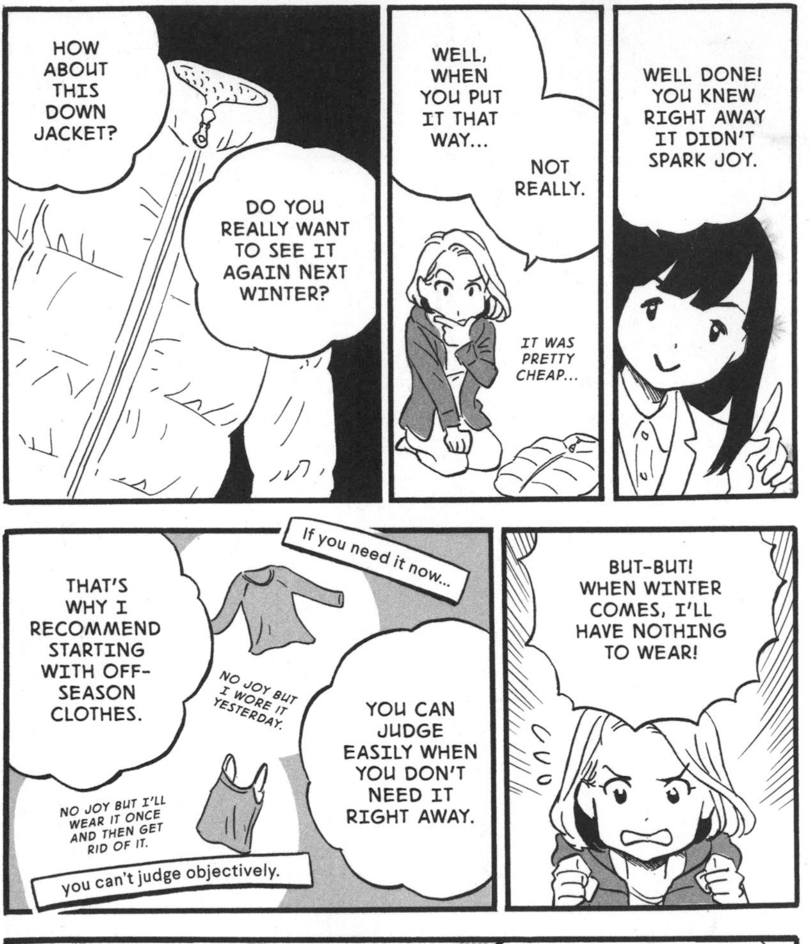
HOW ABOUT THIS DOWN JACKET?
DO YOU REALLY WANT TO SEE IT AGAIN NEXT WINTER?
WELL, WHEN YOU PUT IT THAT WAY...
NOT REALLY.
IT WAS PRETTY CHEAP...
WELL DONE! YOU KNEW RIGHT AWAY IT DIDN'T SPARK JOY.
If you need it now...
THAT'S WHY I RECOMMEND STARTING WITH OFF-SEASON CLOTHES.
NO JOY BUT I WORE IT YESTERDAY.
YOU CAN JUDGE EASILY WHEN YOU DON'T NEED IT RIGHT AWAY.
NO JOY BUT I'LL WEAR IT ONCE AND THEN GET RID OF IT.
you can't judge objectively.
BUT-BUT! WHEN WINTER COMES, I'LL HAVE NOTHING TO WEAR!
DON'T WORRY!
IF YOU KEEP ONLY WHAT SPARKS JOY, YOU'LL HAVE JUST THE AMOUNT YOU NEED.

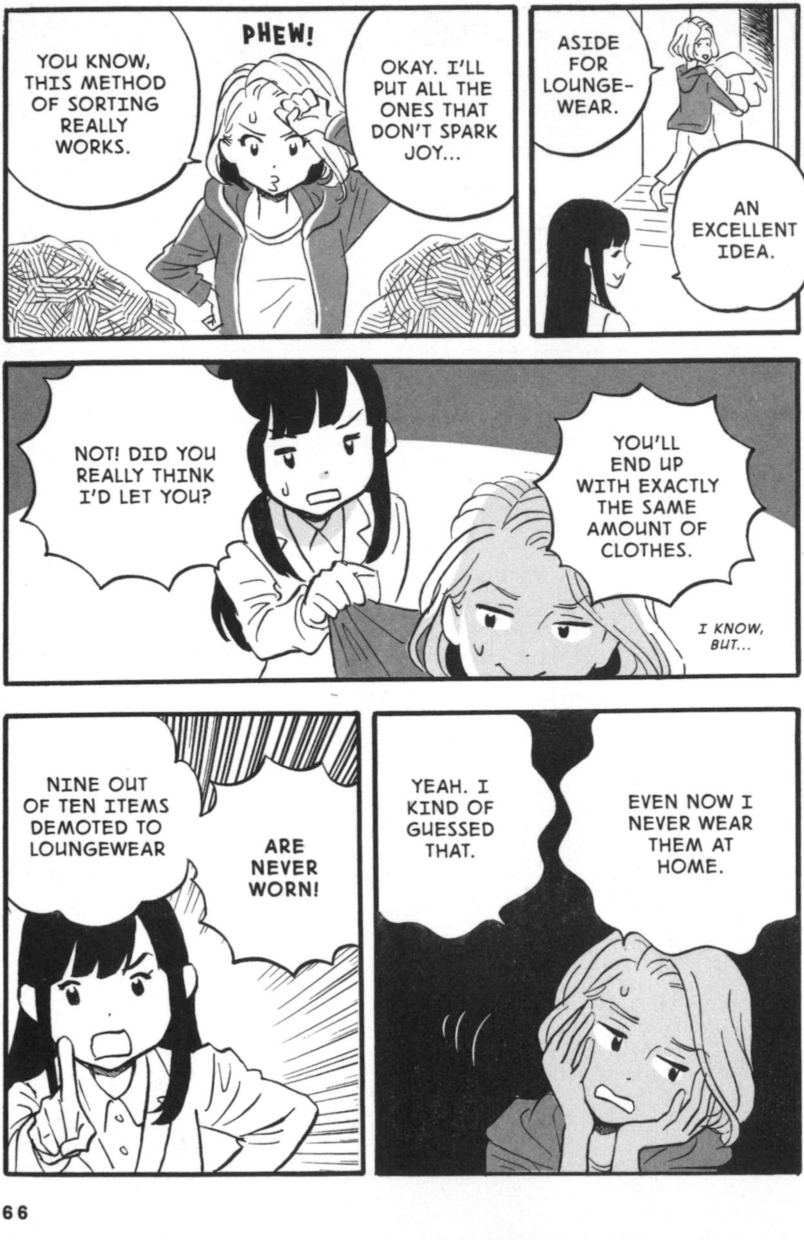
YOU KNOW, THIS METHOD OF SORTING REALLY WORKS.
PHEW!
OKAY. I'LL PUT ALL THE ONES THAT DON'T SPARK JOY...
ASIDE FOR LOUNGE-WEAR.
AN EXCELLENT IDEA.
NOT! DID YOU REALLY THINK I'D LET YOU?
YOU'LL END UP WITH EXACTLY THE SAME AMOUNT OF CLOTHES.
I KNOW, BUT...
NINE OUT OF TEN ITEMS DEMOTED TO LOUNGEWEAR
ARE NEVER WORN!
YEAH. I KIND OF GUESSED THAT.
EVEN NOW I NEVER WEAR THEM AT HOME.

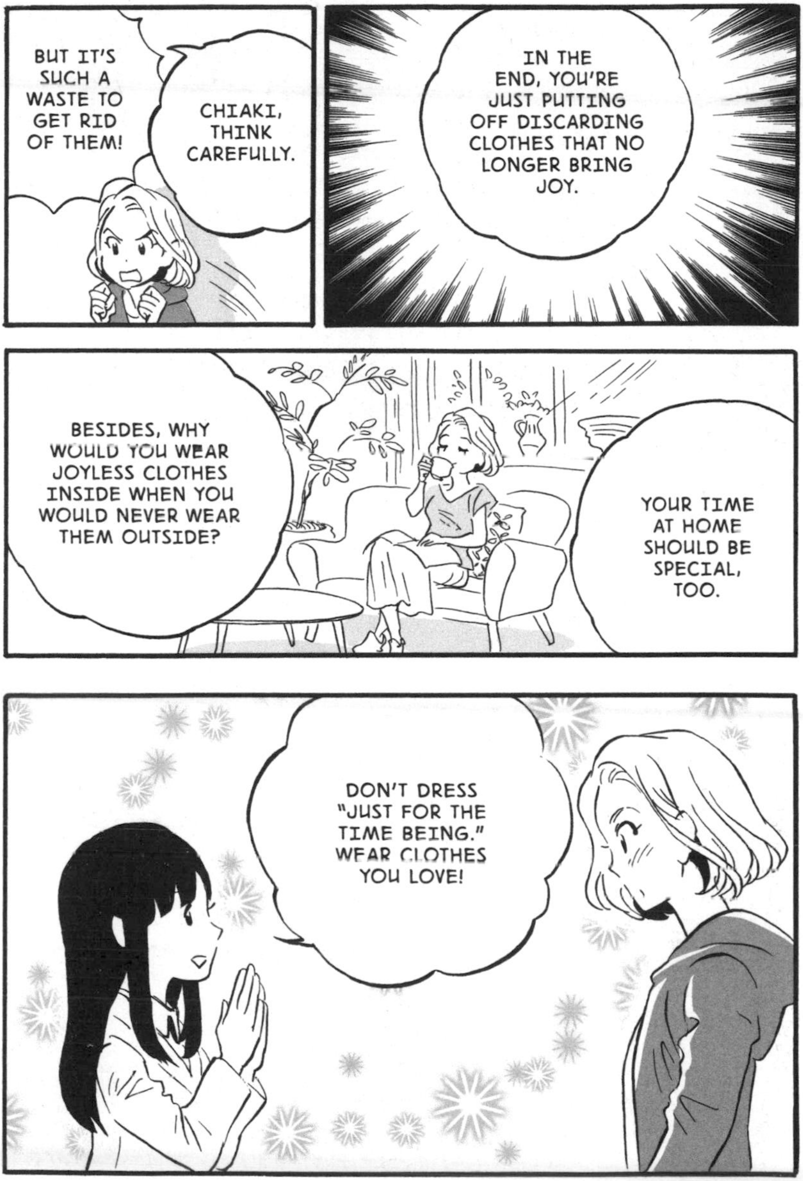
BUT IT'S SUCH A WASTE TO GET RID OF THEM!
CHIAKI, THINK CAREFULLY.
IN THE END, YOU'RE JUST PUTTING OFF DISCARDING CLOTHES THAT NO LONGER BRING JOY.
BESIDES, WHY WOULD YOU WEAR JOYLESS CLOTHES INSIDE WHEN YOU WOULD NEVER WEAR THEM OUTSIDE?
YOUR TIME AT HOME SHOULD BE SPECIAL, TOO.
DON'T DRESS "JUST FOR THE TIME BEING." WEAR CLOTHES YOU LOVE!

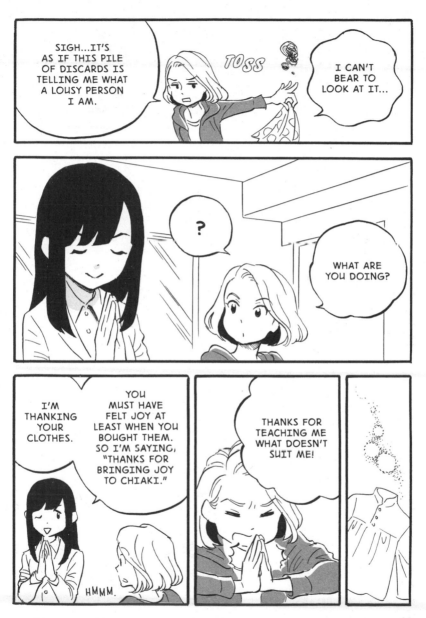

SIGH...IT'S AS IF THIS PILE OF DISCARDS IS TELLING ME WHAT A LOUSY PERSON I AM.

TOSS

I CAN'T BEAR TO LOOK AT IT...

?

WHAT ARE YOU DOING?

I'M THANKING YOUR CLOTHES.

YOU MUST HAVE FELT JOY AT LEAST WHEN YOU BOUGHT THEM. SO I'M SAYING, "THANKS FOR BRINGING JOY TO CHIAKI."

HMMM.

THANKS FOR TEACHING ME WHAT DOESN'T SUIT ME!

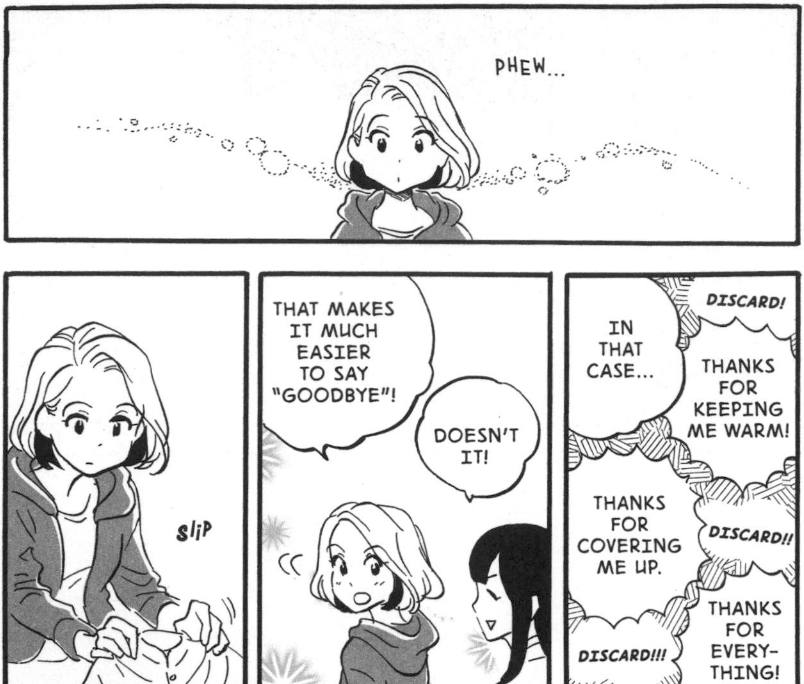
PHEW...
SLIP
THAT MAKES IT MUCH EASIER TO SAY "GOODBYE"!
DOESN'T IT!
IN THAT CASE...
DISCARD!
THANKS FOR KEEPING ME WARM!
THANKS FOR COVERING ME UP.
DISCARD!!
DISCARD!!!
THANKS FOR EVERY-THING!
TUG
THIRTY BAGS!
WELL DONE! KEEP UP THE GOOD WORK!

YOU CAN DONATE THOSE IN GOOD CONDITION TO A CHARITY SHOP OR TAKE THEM TO A RECYCLE STATION.

Don't tidy by place or by room, but by category.

———

Most people can't tidy because they have too much stuff. They accumulate too much stuff because they don't know how much they actually own.

Gather every single item in the category from every corner of your home. Pile them all in one spot. This way, you can see exactly how much you have.

Things that have been put away in a drawer or a closet are basically dormant. Wake them up by taking them out and spreading them across the floor to expose them to the air. When you do, you will be amazed to find that your joy barometer becomes clear and focused.

Gathering everything in the same category in one spot is the best way to finish tidying up quickly.

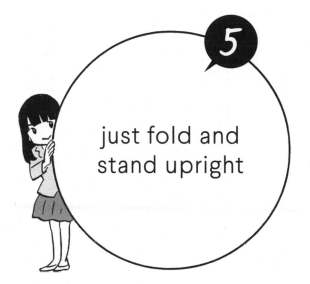

5

just fold and
stand upright

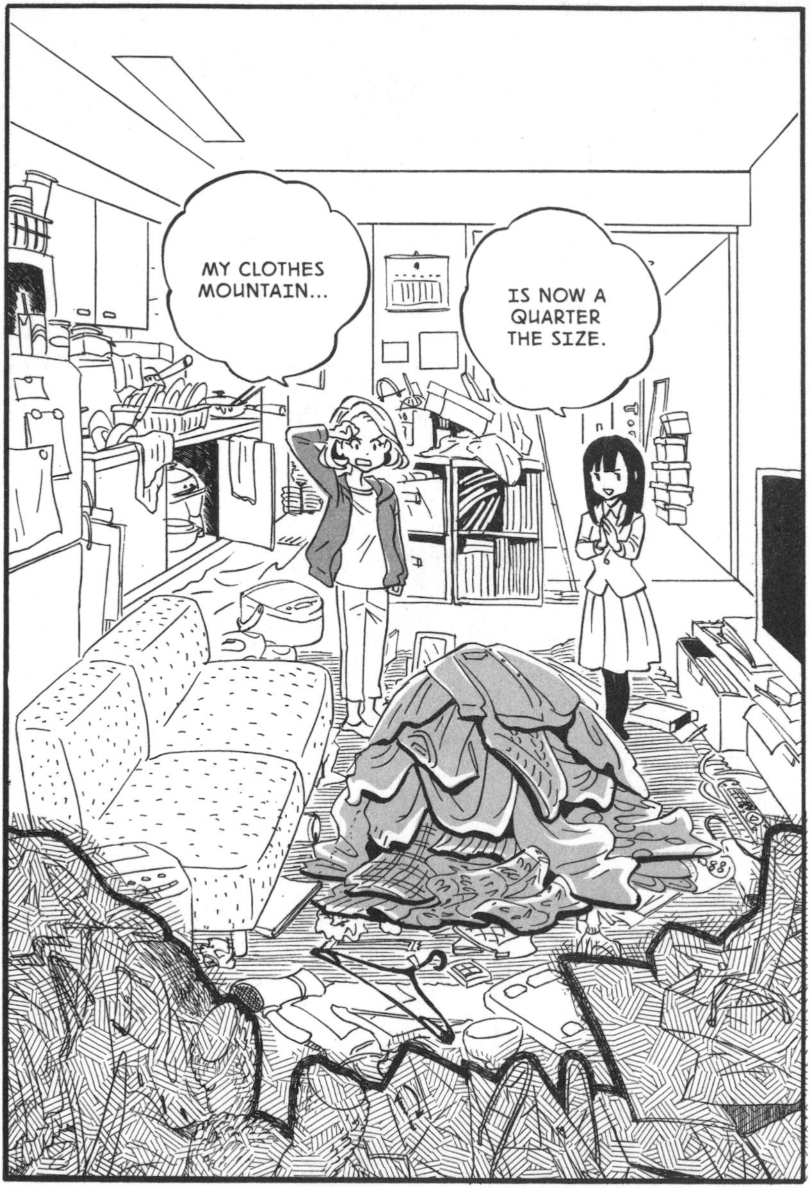
MY CLOTHES MOUNTAIN...
IS NOW A QUARTER THE SIZE.

CLOTHES THAT HAVE BEEN THROWN INTO A DRAWER

CLEARLY DIFFER FROM THOSE THAT HAVE BEEN CAREFULLY FOLDED.

CLOTHES THAT'VE BEEN FOLDED SEEM BRIGHTER AND MORE RESILIENT.

FOLDING OUR CLOTHES IS AN EXPRESSION OF LOVE AND APPRECIATION.

AND OUR CLOTHES WILL RESPOND.

TO FOLD YOUR CLOTHES IS TO CONVERSE WITH THEM.

I SEE. LOVE...

APPRECIATION... CONVERSATION...?

OH! IT'S NO GOOD. I HATE FOLDING!

DON'T WORRY! THAT'S WHY I'M HERE. LET ME GIVE YOU A COMPLETE FOLDING LESSON!

ONCE YOU MASTER THE CORRECT WAY TO FOLD, IT'LL COME NATURALLY,

AND YOU CAN USE IT FOR THE REST OF YOUR LIFE!

FOLDING T-SHIRTS
THERE'S JUST ONE IMPORTANT POINT: AIM TO MAKE A SMOOTH RECTANGLE!
Fold back the sleeve
1.
2.
3.
4.

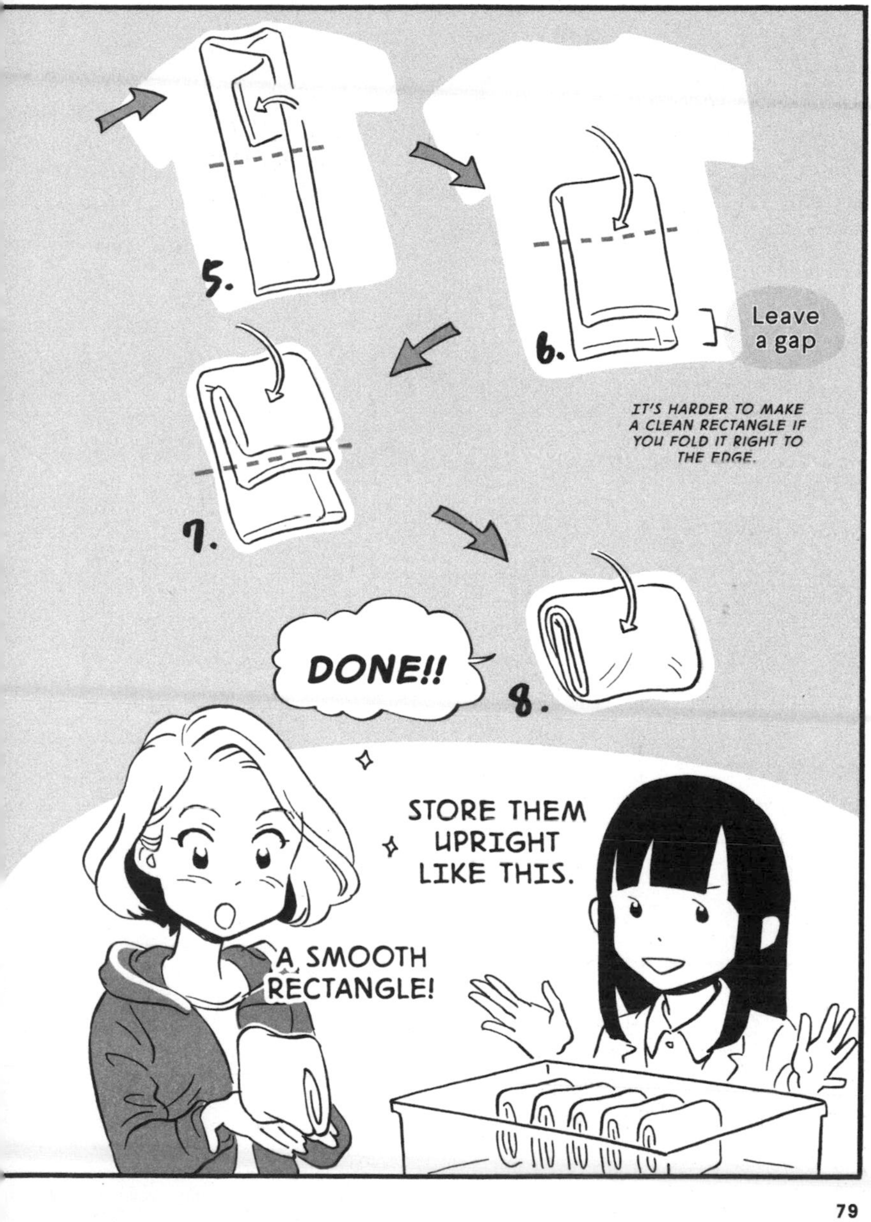

5.
6.
Leave a gap
IT'S HARDER TO MAKE A CLEAN RECTANGLE IF YOU FOLD IT RIGHT TO THE EDGE.
7.
DONE!!
8.
A SMOOTH RECTANGLE!
STORE THEM UPRIGHT LIKE THIS.

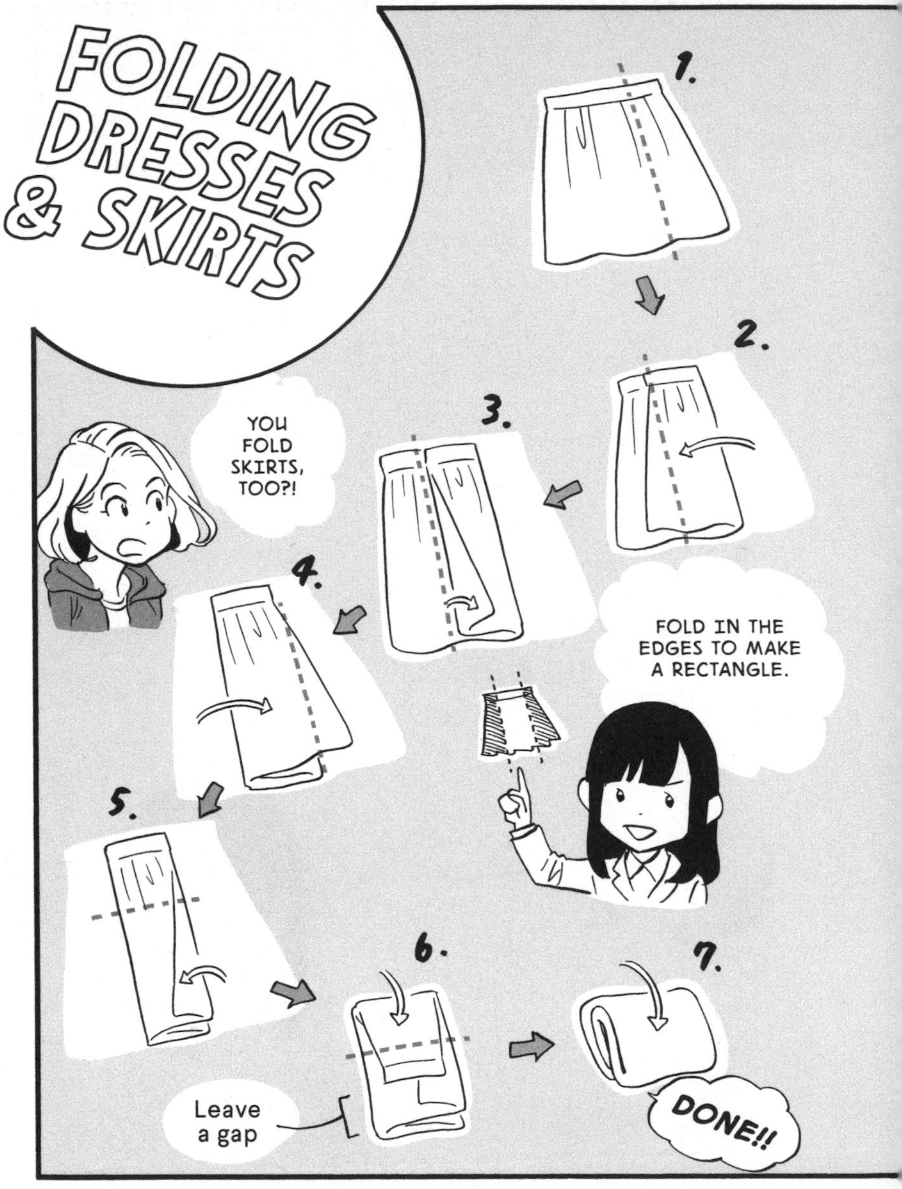
FOLDING DRESSES & SKIRTS
1.
2.
3.
YOU FOLD SKIRTS, TOO?!
4.
FOLD IN THE EDGES TO MAKE A RECTANGLE.
5.
6.
7.
Leave a gap
DONE!!

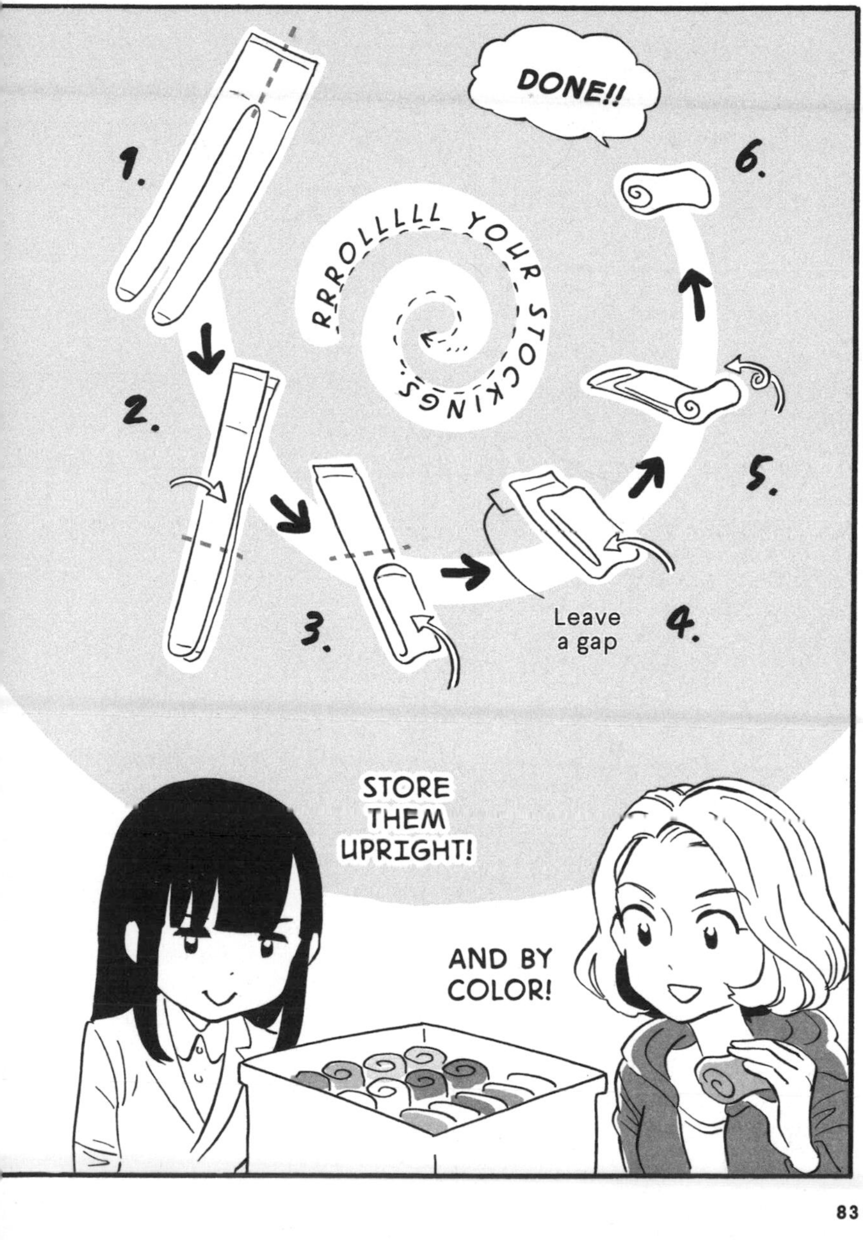
1.
2.
3.
4.
5.
6.
DONE!!
RRROLLLLL YOUR STOCKINGS.
Leave a gap
STORE THEM UPRIGHT!
AND BY COLOR!

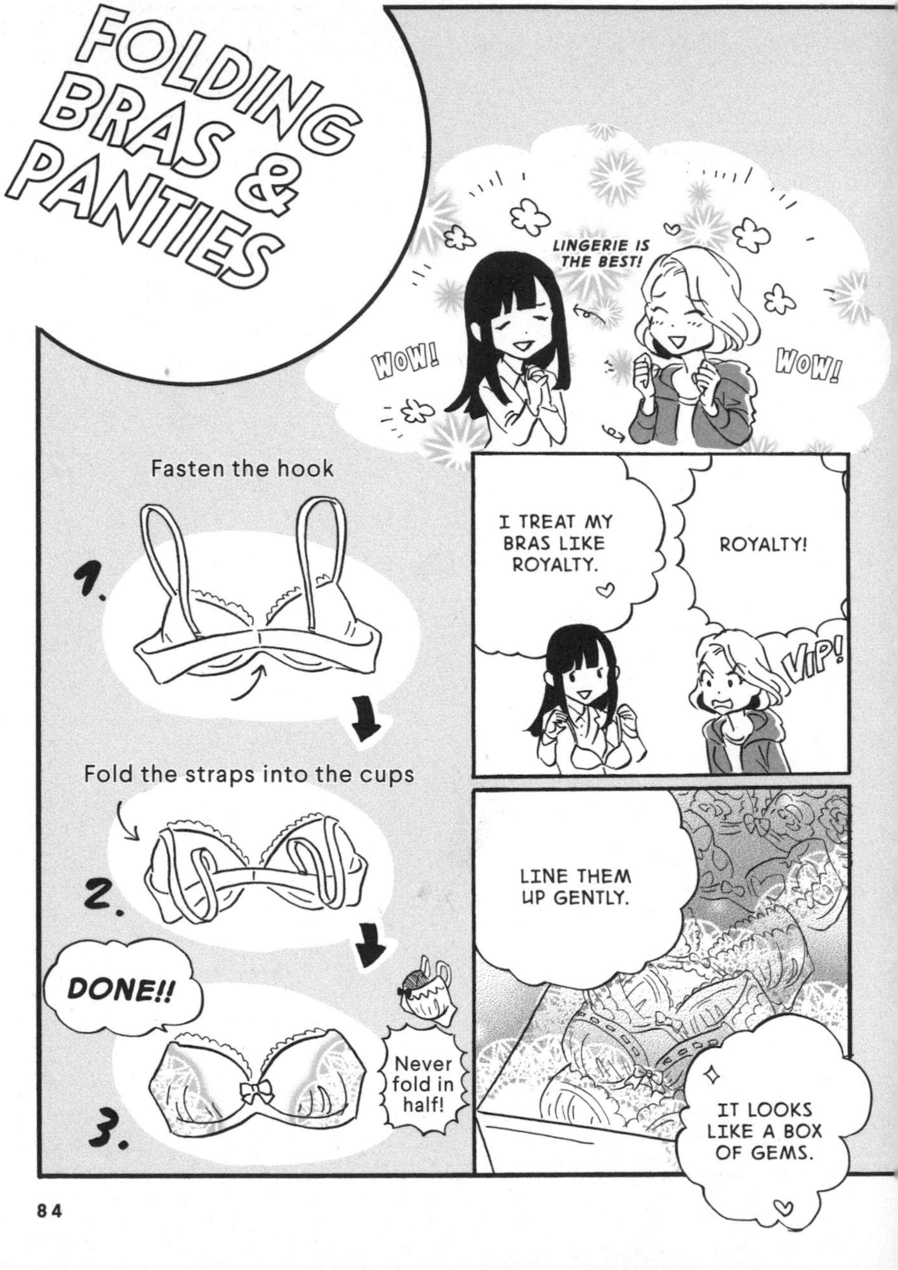
FOLDING BRAS & PANTIES
LINGERIE IS THE BEST!
WOW!
WOW!
Fasten the hook
1.
Fold the straps into the cups
2.
DONE!!
3.
Never fold in half!
I TREAT MY BRAS LIKE ROYALTY.
ROYALTY!
VIP!
LINE THEM UP GENTLY.
IT LOOKS LIKE A BOX OF GEMS.

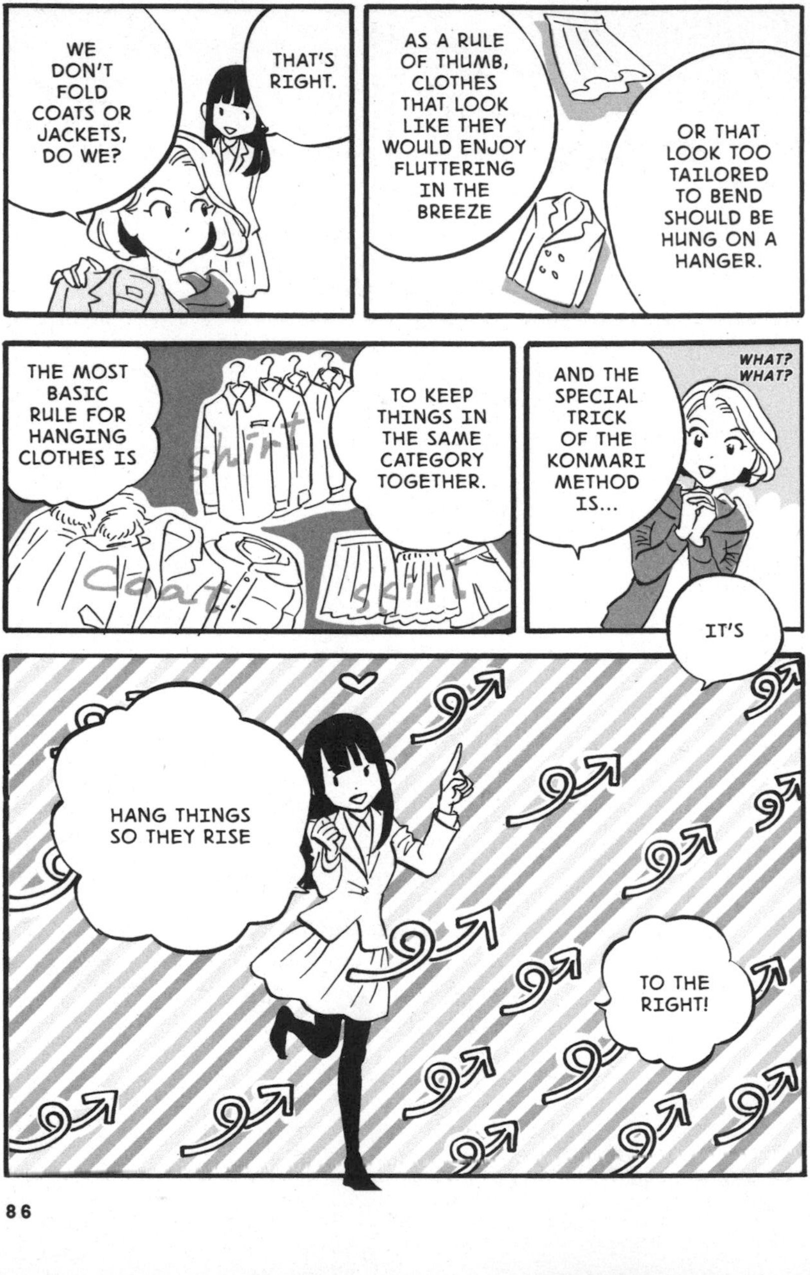
WE DON'T FOLD COATS OR JACKETS, DO WE?
THAT'S RIGHT.
AS A RULE OF THUMB, CLOTHES THAT LOOK LIKE THEY WOULD ENJOY FLUTTERING IN THE BREEZE
OR THAT LOOK TOO TAILORED TO BEND SHOULD BE HUNG ON A HANGER.
THE MOST BASIC RULE FOR HANGING CLOTHES IS
shirt
coat
skirt
TO KEEP THINGS IN THE SAME CATEGORY TOGETHER.
AND THE SPECIAL TRICK OF THE KONMARI METHOD IS...
WHAT? WHAT?
IT'S
HANG THINGS SO THEY RISE
TO THE RIGHT!

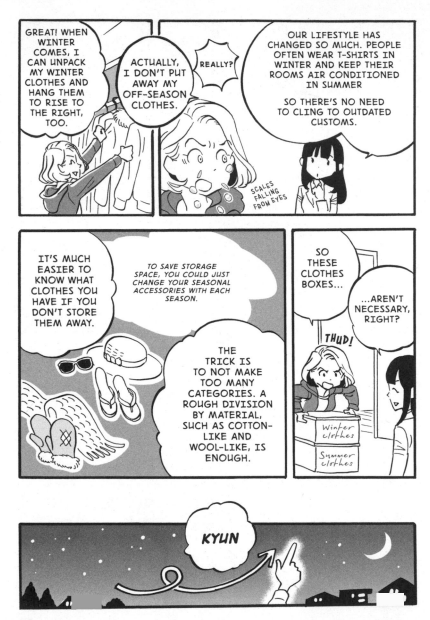

Folding your clothes is an opportunity to show them your appreciation for all they do to support your life.

─────

Do you think folding clothes and storing them in a drawer is a pain? Would you rather just hang them all in the closet? If so, you don't know the power of folding.

Folding can solve almost all your clothing storage problems. But the real value of folding is this: By touching your clothes with your hands, you pass on your energy. Try folding your clothes with gratitude in your heart for the way they protect you.

6

choose
books
by feel

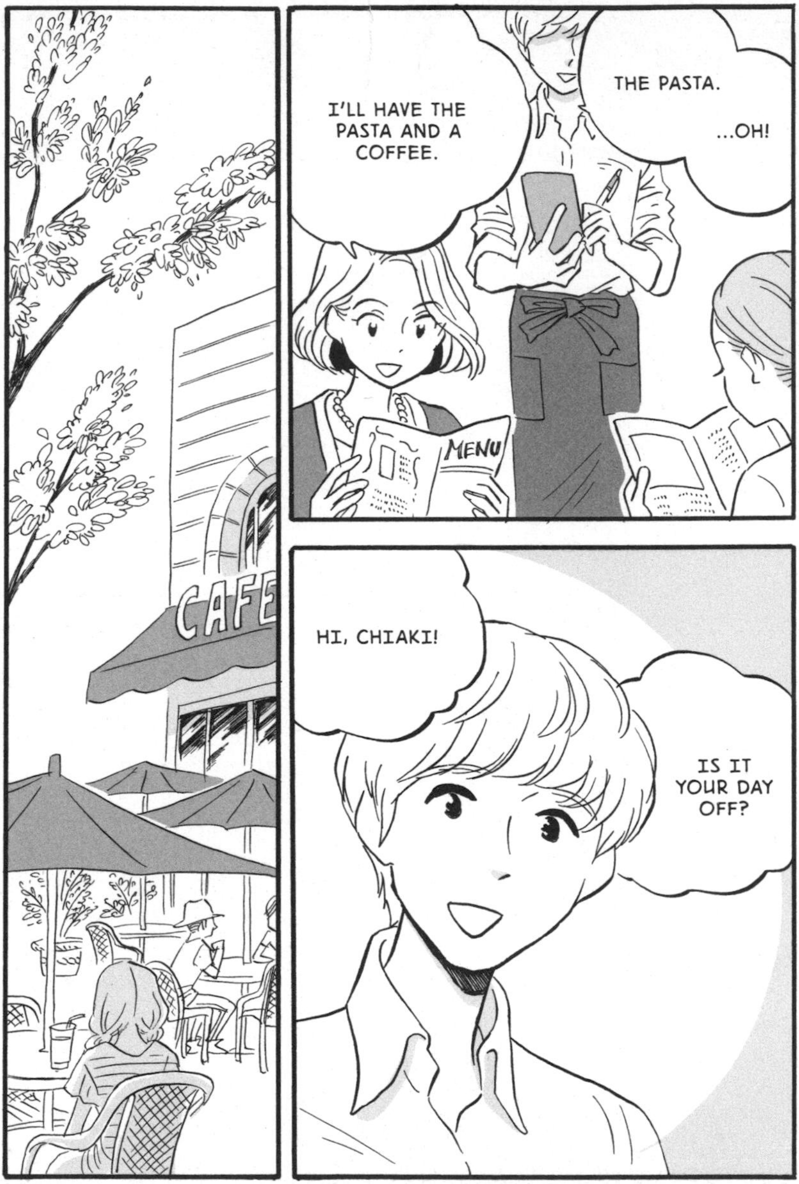
CAFE
I'LL HAVE THE PASTA AND A COFFEE.
THE PASTA.
...OH!
MENU
HI, CHIAKI!
IS IT YOUR DAY OFF?

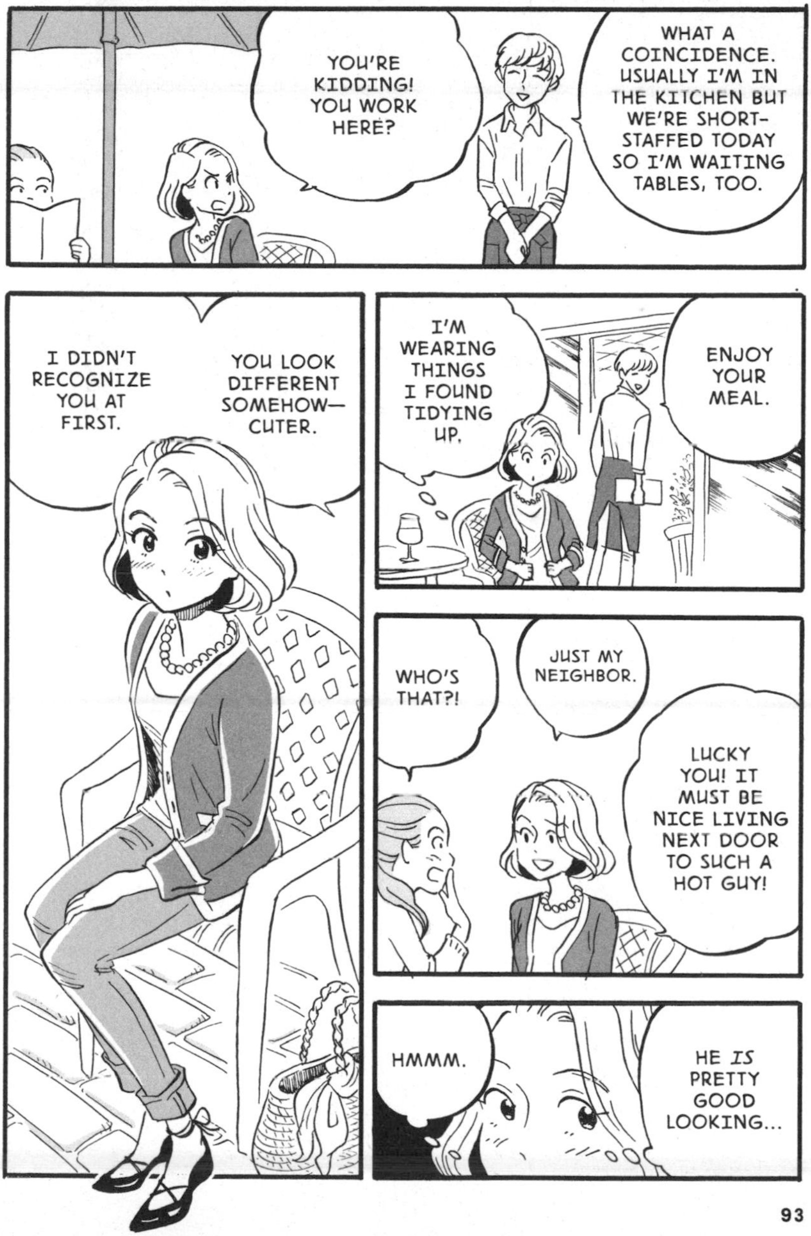
YOU'RE KIDDING! YOU WORK HERE?
WHAT A COINCIDENCE. USUALLY I'M IN THE KITCHEN BUT WE'RE SHORT-STAFFED TODAY SO I'M WAITING TABLES, TOO.
I DIDN'T RECOGNIZE YOU AT FIRST.
YOU LOOK DIFFERENT SOMEHOW—CUTER.
I'M WEARING THINGS I FOUND TIDYING UP.
ENJOY YOUR MEAL.
WHO'S THAT?!
JUST MY NEIGHBOR.
LUCKY YOU! IT MUST BE NICE LIVING NEXT DOOR TO SUCH A HOT GUY!
HMMM.
HE *IS* PRETTY GOOD LOOKING...

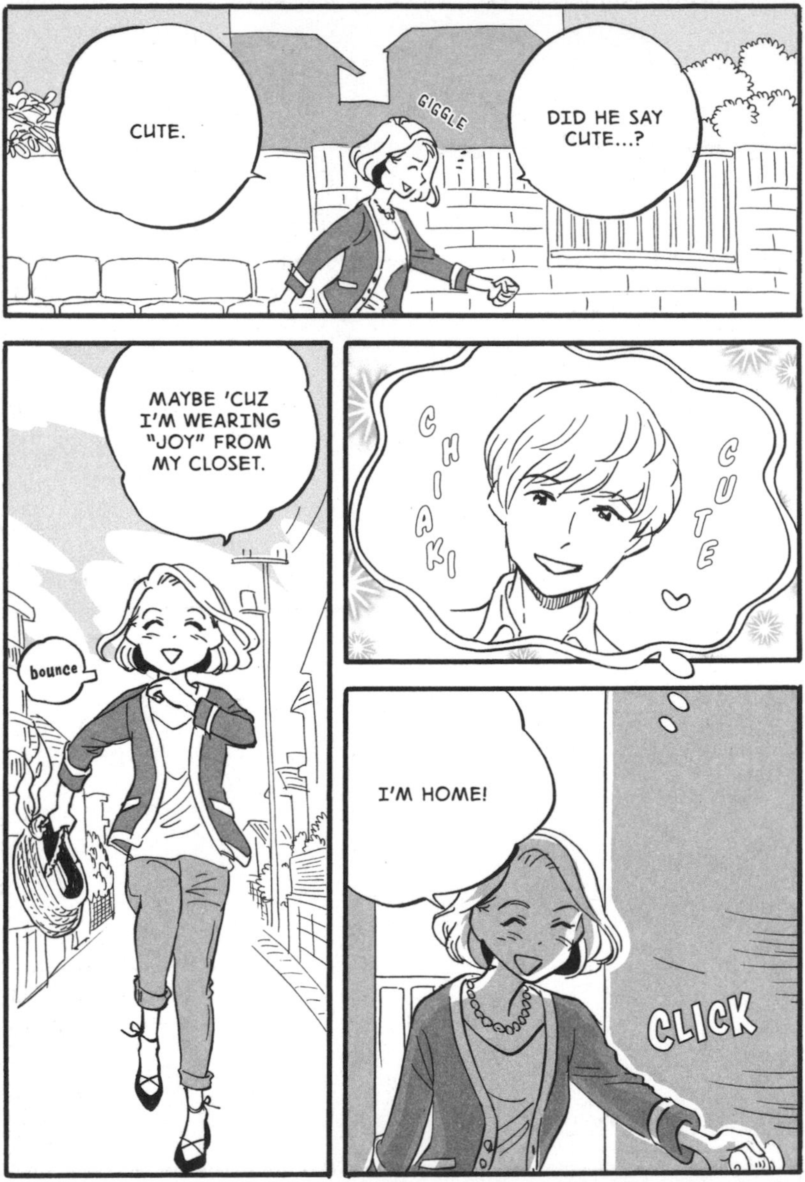
CUTE.
GIGGLE
DID HE SAY CUTE...?
MAYBE 'CUZ I'M WEARING "JOY" FROM MY CLOSET.
bounce
CHIAKI
CUTE
CUTE
I'M HOME!
CLICK

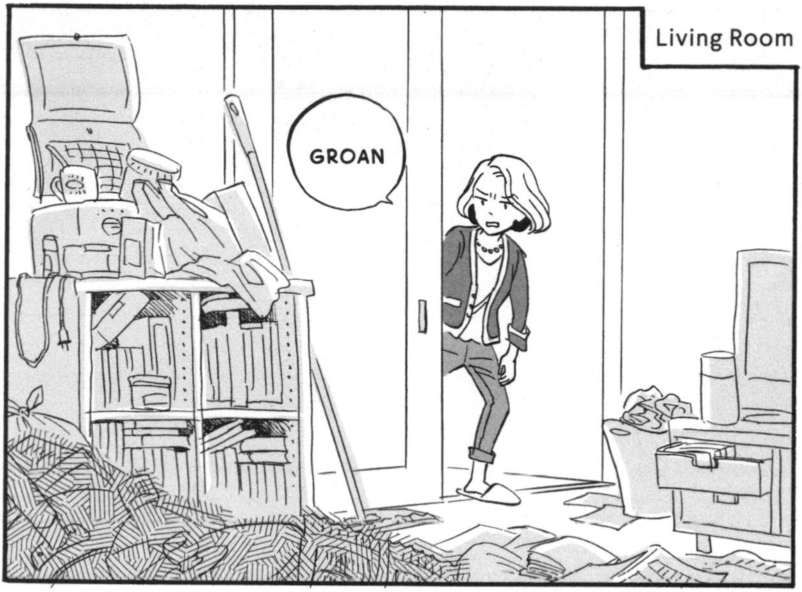
Living Room
GROAN

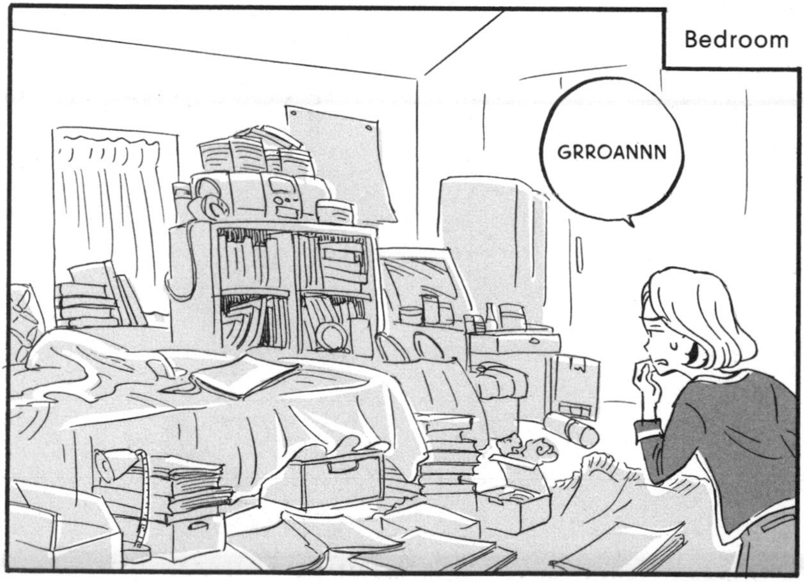
Bedroom
GRROANNN

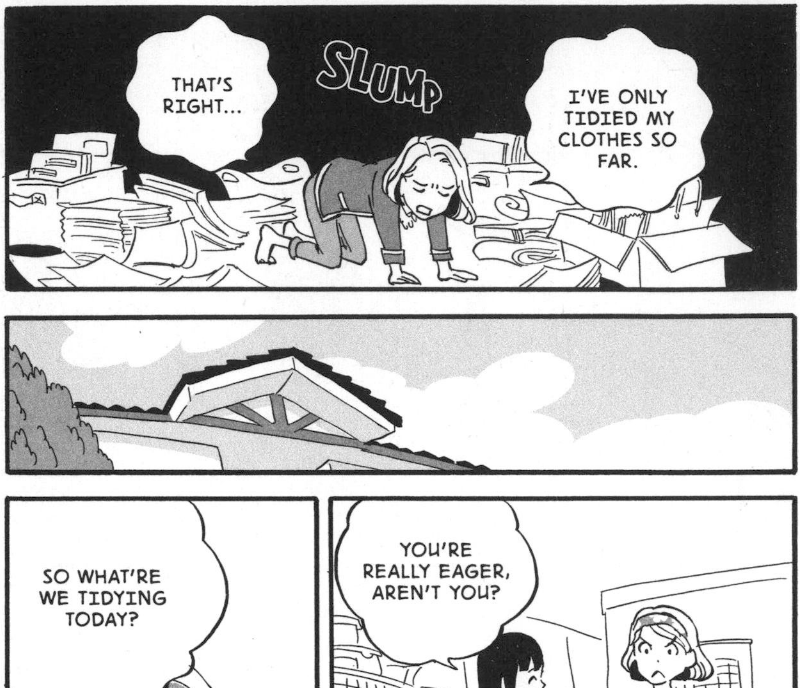
THAT'S RIGHT...
SLUMP
I'VE ONLY TIDIED MY CLOTHES SO FAR.
SO WHAT'RE WE TIDYING TODAY?
YOU'RE REALLY EAGER, AREN'T YOU?
TODAY WE'LL TIDY...
BOOKS!

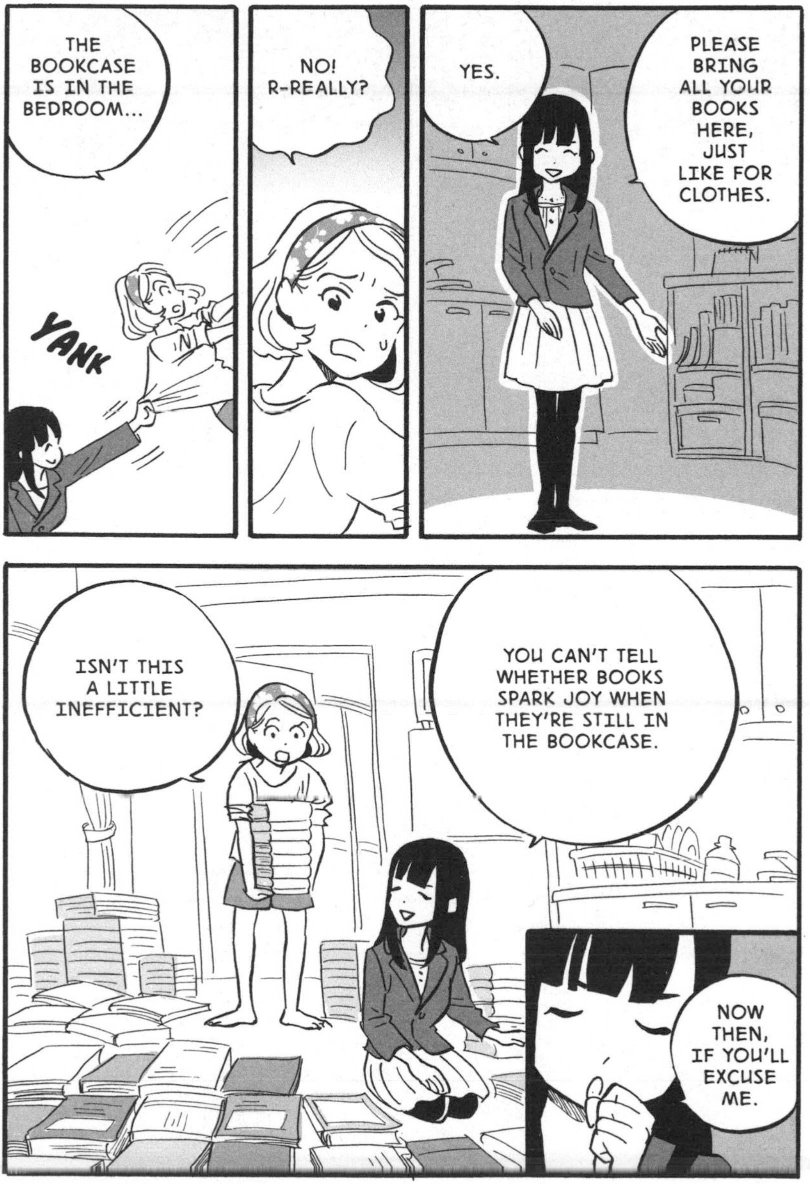
THE BOOKCASE IS IN THE BEDROOM...
YANK
NO! R-REALLY?
YES.
PLEASE BRING ALL YOUR BOOKS HERE, JUST LIKE FOR CLOTHES.
ISN'T THIS A LITTLE INEFFICIENT?
YOU CAN'T TELL WHETHER BOOKS SPARK JOY WHEN THEY'RE STILL IN THE BOOKCASE.
NOW THEN, IF YOU'LL EXCUSE ME.

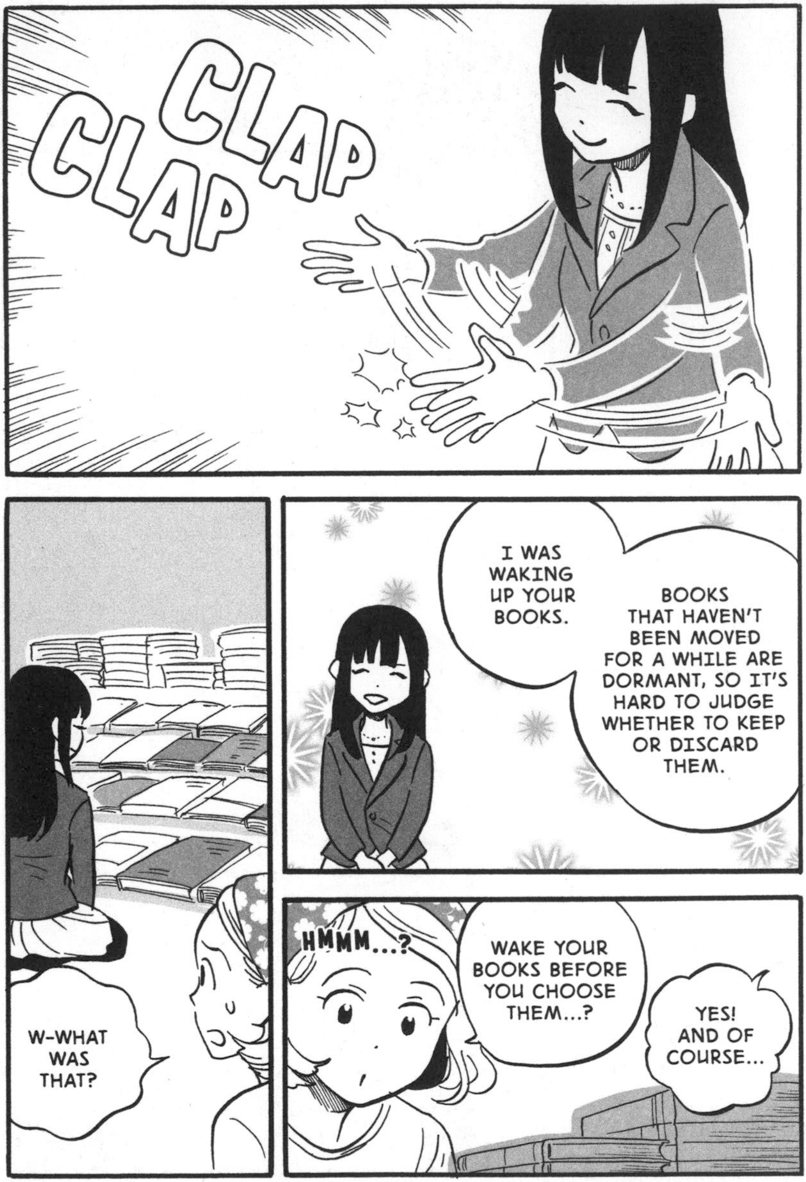

CLAP CLAP
W-WHAT WAS THAT?
I WAS WAKING UP YOUR BOOKS.
BOOKS THAT HAVEN'T BEEN MOVED FOR A WHILE ARE DORMANT, SO IT'S HARD TO JUDGE WHETHER TO KEEP OR DISCARD THEM.
HMMM...?
WAKE YOUR BOOKS BEFORE YOU CHOOSE THEM...?
YES! AND OF COURSE...

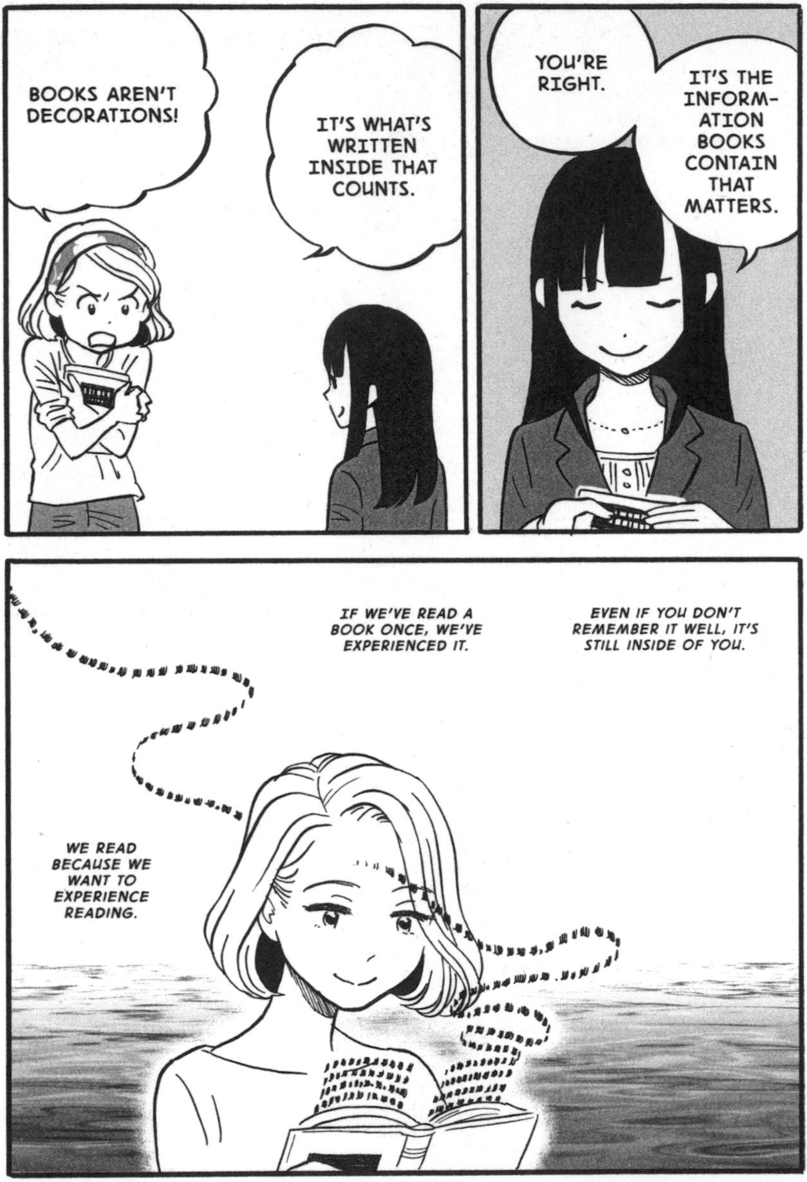
BOOKS AREN'T DECORATIONS!
IT'S WHAT'S WRITTEN INSIDE THAT COUNTS.
YOU'RE RIGHT.
IT'S THE INFORM-ATION BOOKS CONTAIN THAT MATTERS.
IF WE'VE READ A BOOK ONCE, WE'VE EXPERIENCED IT.
EVEN IF YOU DON'T REMEMBER IT WELL, IT'S STILL INSIDE OF YOU.
WE READ BECAUSE WE WANT TO EXPERIENCE READING.

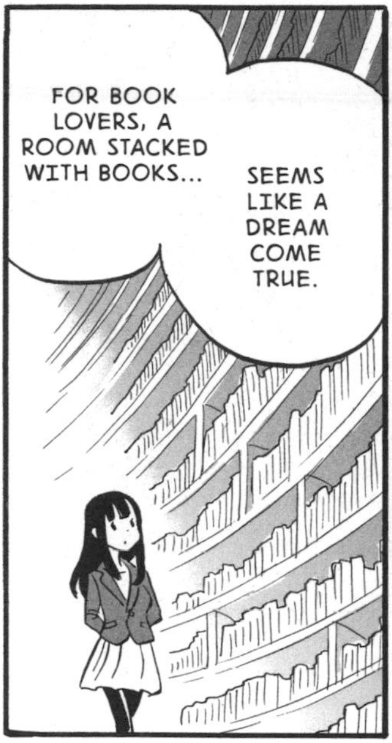
FOR BOOK LOVERS, A ROOM STACKED WITH BOOKS...
SEEMS LIKE A DREAM COME TRUE.

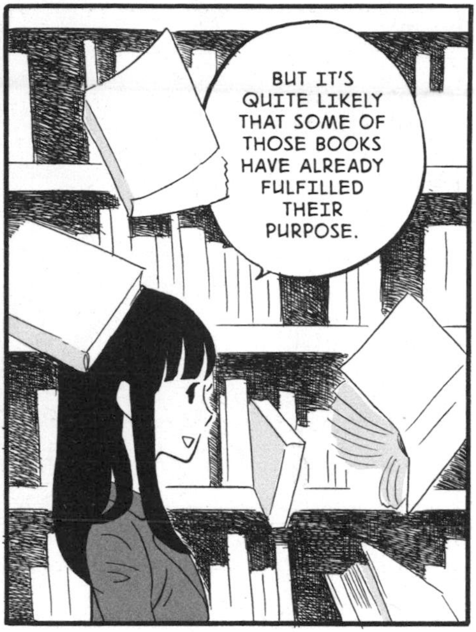
BUT IT'S QUITE LIKELY THAT SOME OF THOSE BOOKS HAVE ALREADY FULFILLED THEIR PURPOSE.

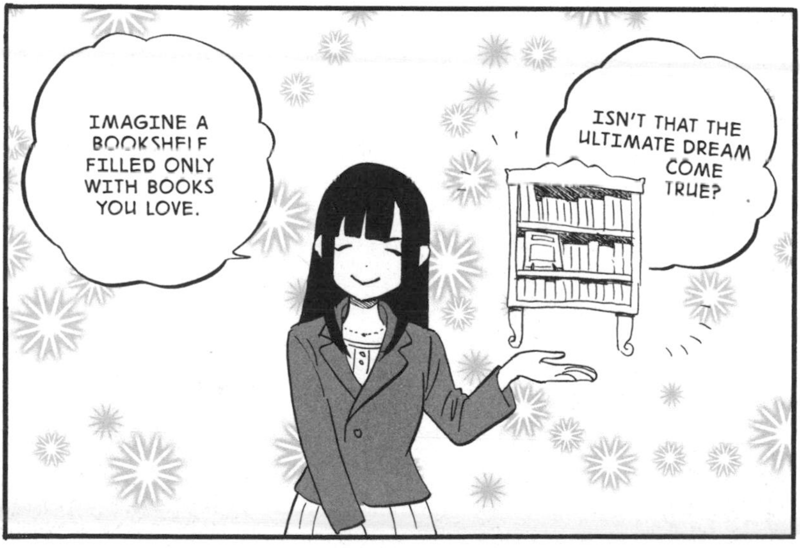
IMAGINE A BOOKSHELF FILLED ONLY WITH BOOKS YOU LOVE.
ISN'T THAT THE ULTIMATE DREAM COME TRUE?

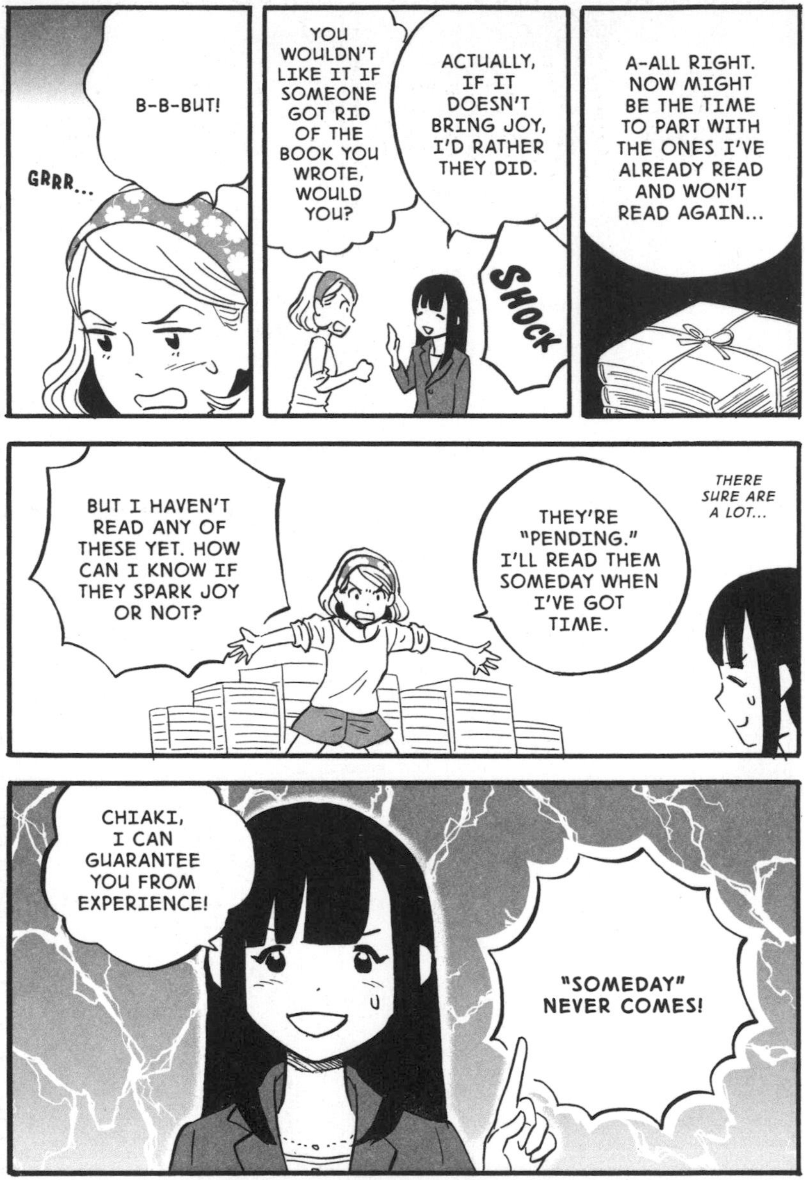
B-B-BUT!
GRRR...
YOU WOULDN'T LIKE IT IF SOMEONE GOT RID OF THE BOOK YOU WROTE, WOULD YOU?
ACTUALLY, IF IT DOESN'T BRING JOY, I'D RATHER THEY DID.
SHOCK
A-ALL RIGHT. NOW MIGHT BE THE TIME TO PART WITH THE ONES I'VE ALREADY READ AND WON'T READ AGAIN...
BUT I HAVEN'T READ ANY OF THESE YET. HOW CAN I KNOW IF THEY SPARK JOY OR NOT?
THEY'RE "PENDING." I'LL READ THEM SOMEDAY WHEN I'VE GOT TIME.
THERE SURE ARE A LOT...
CHIAKI, I CAN GUARANTEE YOU FROM EXPERIENCE!
"SOMEDAY" NEVER COMES!

IF YOU'VE MISSED THE RIGHT TIMING FOR READING A BOOK,

INCLUDING RECOMMENDED BOOKS OR ONES ON YOUR TO-READ LIST, NOW'S THE TIME TO LET GO.

RECOMMENDED

UNREAD

ONLINE FAVORITE

UNREAD

SO DONATE YOUR UNREAD BOOKS!

DON'T WORRY! THEY'LL COME BACK TO YOU IF THEY'RE MEANT TO.

Tr secondhand bookstore

CHIAKI, YOU SURE HAVE A LOT OF TEXT-BOOKS.

Bookkeeping Level 3

FP Skill Training

Nutritionist

Aromatherapy Levels 1 & 2

TOEIC in 3 Weeks

ER, WELL...

I WAS GOING TO STUDY THEM SOMEDAY.

IT MIGHT BE HANDY TO HAVE LANGUAGE OR BOOKKEEPING SKILLS, YOU KNOW.

IF YOU NEVER GOT PAST JUST THINKING ABOUT IT, SAY "GOODBYE" FOR NOW.

YEAH, YOU'RE RIGHT...

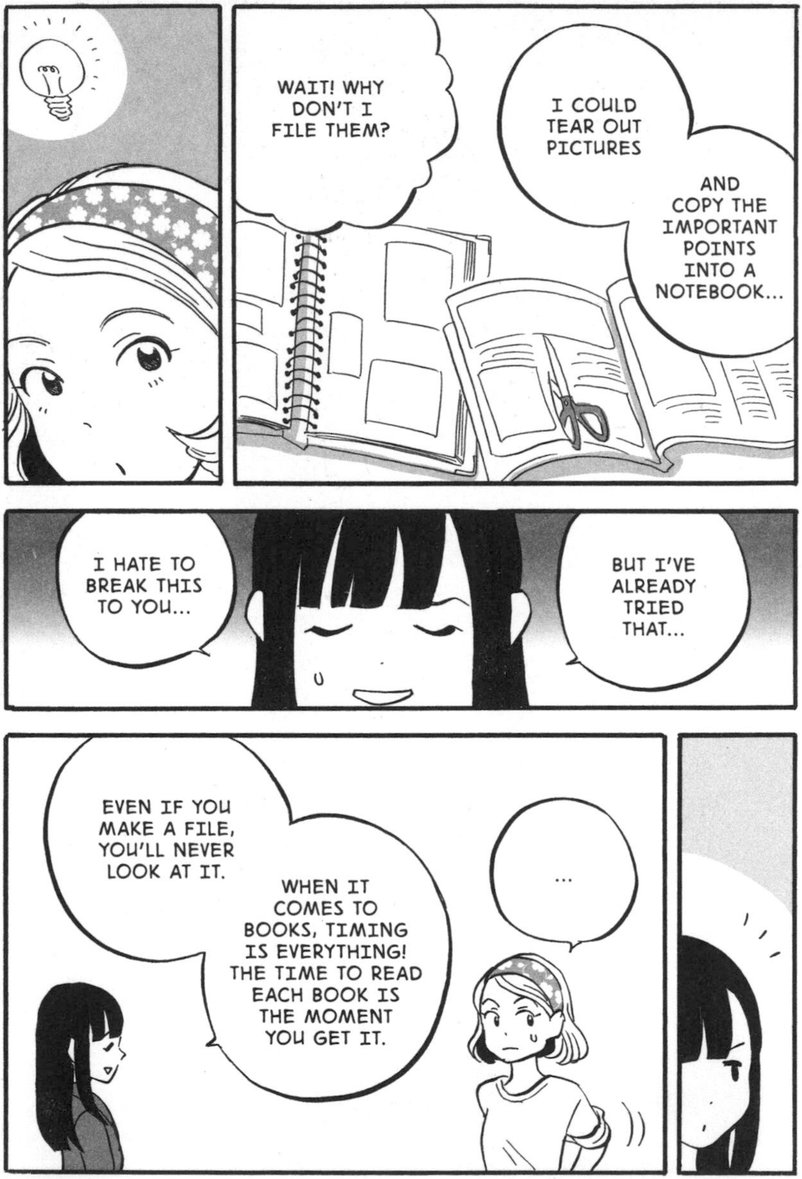
WAIT! WHY DON'T I FILE THEM?
I COULD TEAR OUT PICTURES
AND COPY THE IMPORTANT POINTS INTO A NOTEBOOK...
I HATE TO BREAK THIS TO YOU...
BUT I'VE ALREADY TRIED THAT...
EVEN IF YOU MAKE A FILE, YOU'LL NEVER LOOK AT IT.
WHEN IT COMES TO BOOKS, TIMING IS EVERYTHING! THE TIME TO READ EACH BOOK IS THE MOMENT YOU GET IT.
...

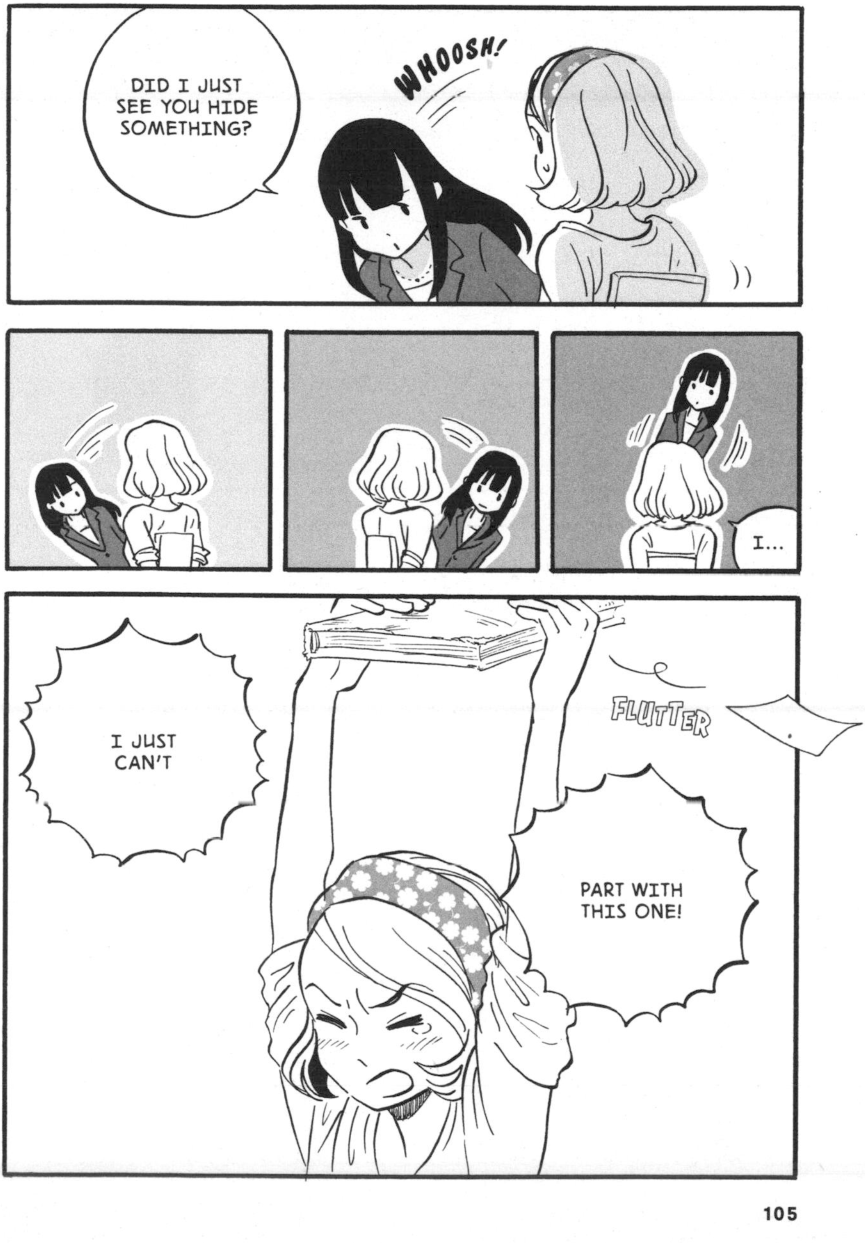
DID I JUST SEE YOU HIDE SOMETHING?
WHOOSH!
I...
I JUST CAN'T
FLUTTER
PART WITH THIS ONE!

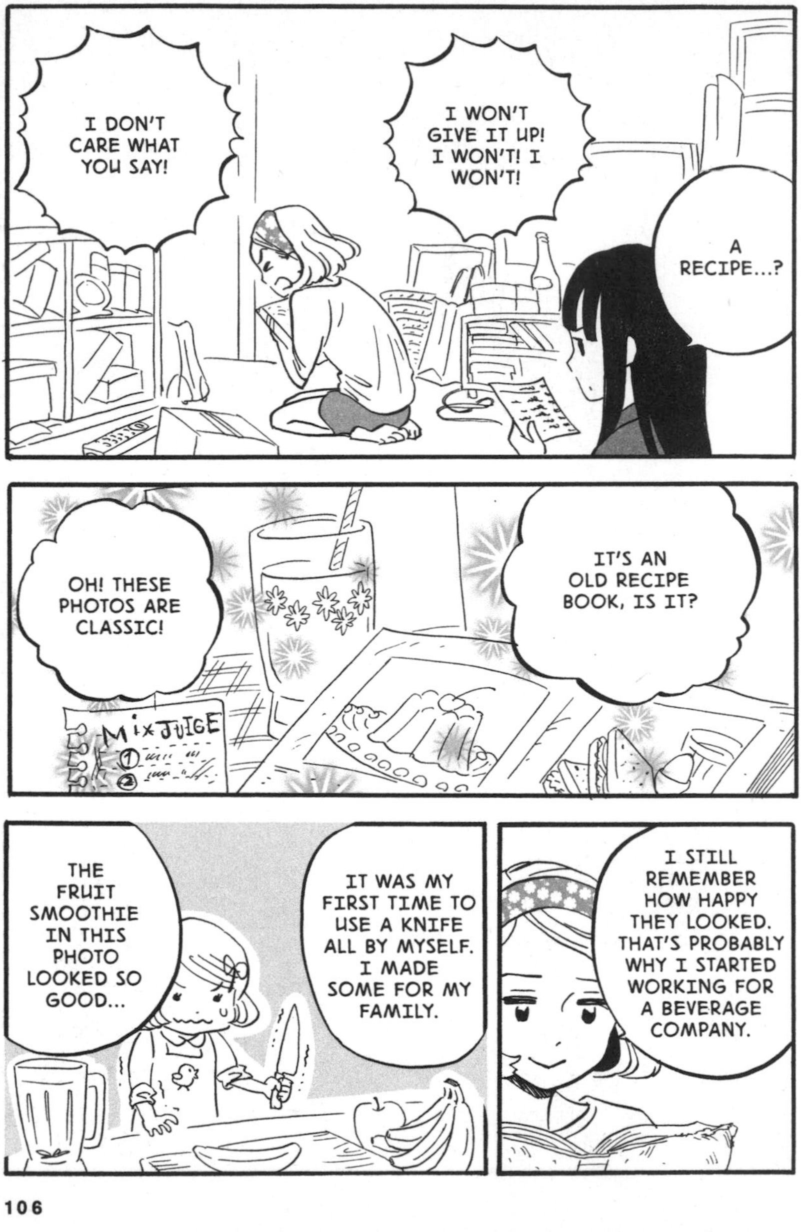
I DON'T CARE WHAT YOU SAY!
I WON'T GIVE IT UP! I WON'T! I WON'T!
A RECIPE...?
OH! THESE PHOTOS ARE CLASSIC!
IT'S AN OLD RECIPE BOOK, IS IT?
MIX JUICE
THE FRUIT SMOOTHIE IN THIS PHOTO LOOKED SO GOOD...
IT WAS MY FIRST TIME TO USE A KNIFE ALL BY MYSELF. I MADE SOME FOR MY FAMILY.
I STILL REMEMBER HOW HAPPY THEY LOOKED. THAT'S PROBABLY WHY I STARTED WORKING FOR A BEVERAGE COMPANY.

Do you have unread books that
you intend to read "someday"?
Believe me. "Someday" never
comes.

———

Take all your books off the shelf and
put them on the floor. Pick them
up one by one and choose which
ones you want to keep. Of course,
the criterion is whether or not they
spark joy. Keep those that belong
in your personal Hall of Fame and
treasure them.

Take this opportunity to get rid of
all your unread, neglected books.
When you're left with only those
that spark joy, you'll find that the
quality of information that comes
your way changes dramatically.

By discarding books, you create
space for an equivalent amount of
information, and you'll soon see that
the information you need comes
right when you need it.

7

papers and
komono

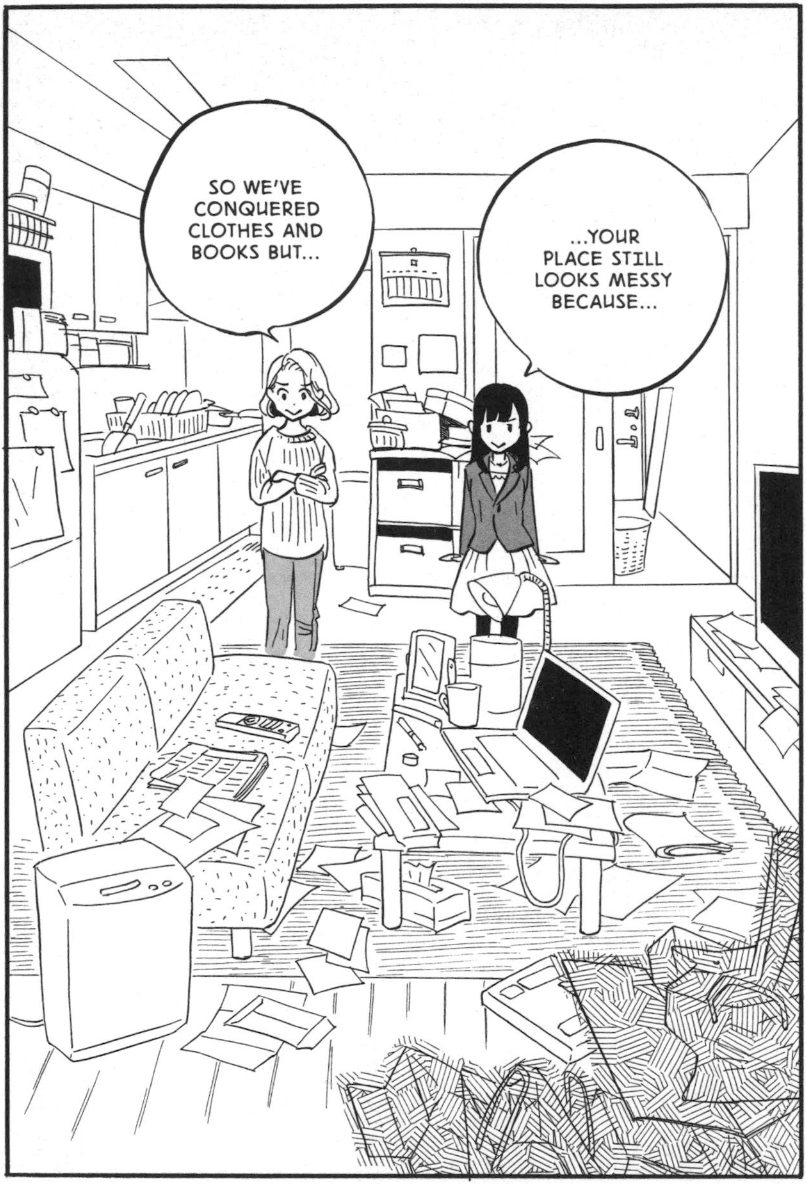
SO WE'VE CONQUERED CLOTHES AND BOOKS BUT...
...YOUR PLACE STILL LOOKS MESSY BECAUSE...

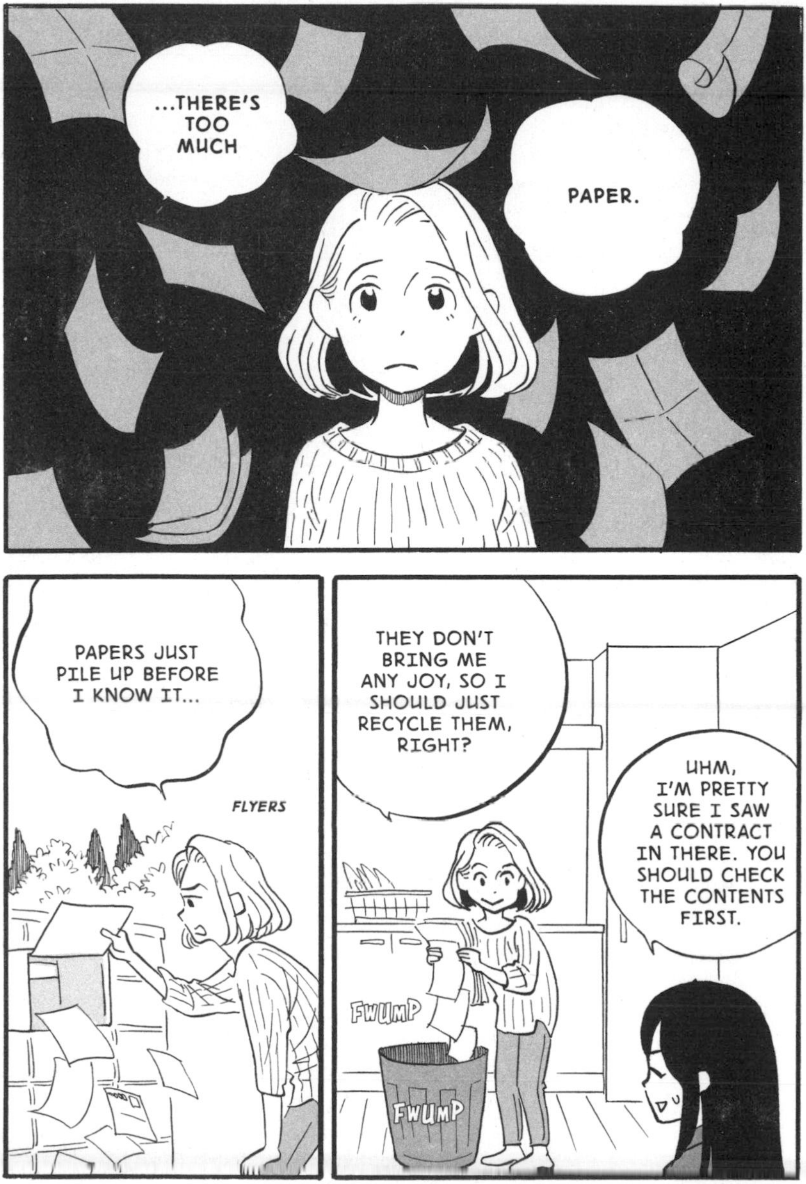
...THERE'S TOO MUCH
PAPER.
PAPERS JUST PILE UP BEFORE I KNOW IT...
FLYERS
THEY DON'T BRING ME ANY JOY, SO I SHOULD JUST RECYCLE THEM, RIGHT?
UHM, I'M PRETTY SURE I SAW A CONTRACT IN THERE. YOU SHOULD CHECK THE CONTENTS FIRST.
FWUMP
FWUMP

BUT, YES, IN THE END...

THE RULE OF THUMB IS TO DISCARD THEM ALL.

SEE?

I KNEW IT!

ON THE TV, THE TABLE...I SEEM TO LEAVE PAPERS EVERYWHERE.

PAPERS ACTUALLY TEND TO PILE UP IN CERTAIN PLACES, LIKE SNOWDRIFTS.

PEOPLE OFTEN THINK A HOME HAS LESS PAPER THAN AN OFFICE,

BUT WHEN YOU GATHER THEM ALL TOGETHER, THERE'S QUITE A LOT.

SHREDDER GOING FULL BLAST

ONE OF MY CLIENTS HAD FIFTEEN BAGS OF PAPER RECYCLING.

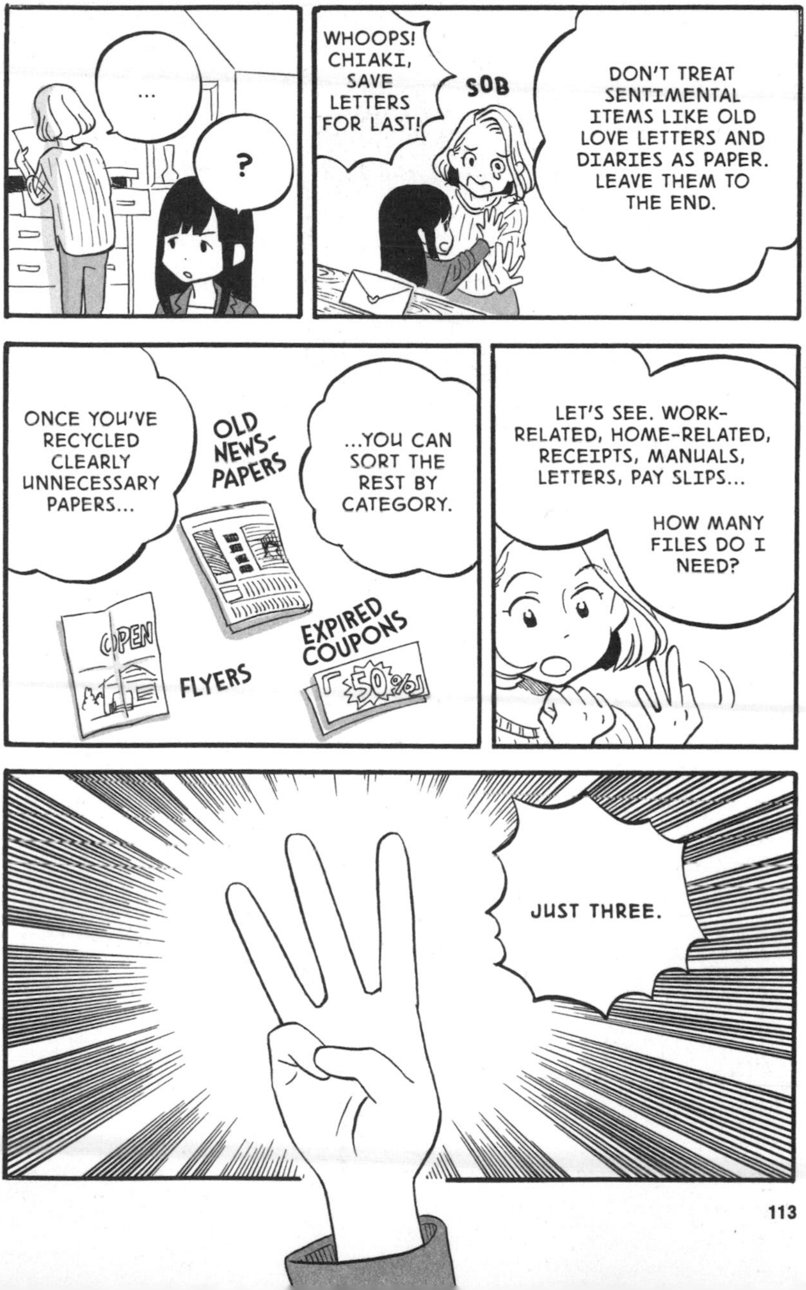
...
?
WHOOPS! CHIAKI, SAVE LETTERS FOR LAST!
SOB
DON'T TREAT SENTIMENTAL ITEMS LIKE OLD LOVE LETTERS AND DIARIES AS PAPER. LEAVE THEM TO THE END.
ONCE YOU'VE RECYCLED CLEARLY UNNECESSARY PAPERS...
OLD NEWS-PAPERS
...YOU CAN SORT THE REST BY CATEGORY.
OPEN
FLYERS
EXPIRED COUPONS
50%
LET'S SEE. WORK-RELATED, HOME-RELATED, RECEIPTS, MANUALS, LETTERS, PAY SLIPS...
HOW MANY FILES DO I NEED?
JUST THREE.

THREE?
YES. YOU CAN USE UP TO THREE FOLDERS OR CONTAINERS.
Needs Attention
Save (contractual)
Save (other)
JUST THESE THREE.
I GET THE FIRST ONE—PENDING.
LETTERS I NEED TO ANSWER, RECEIPTS FOR MY BUDGET...
PLOP PLOP
THE IDEAL IS TO KEEP THIS BOX EMPTY.
I DON'T ALWAYS MAN-AGE IT MYSELF.
I'M NOT SURE ABOUT CATEGORIES TWO AND THREE, "CONTRACTUAL" AND "OTHER."

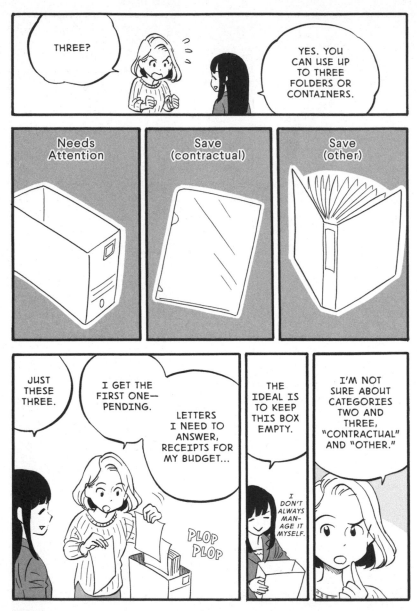

THEY'RE DIVIDED BY FREQUENCY OF USE. CONTRACT-RELATED PAPERS ARE USED THE LEAST.

Lease

Warranty

YOU HARDLY EVER LOOK AT THESE, RIGHT?

Lease contract

Insurance Policy

PUT THEM ALL IN ONE CLEAR PLASTIC FILE.

IT'S THAT SIMPLE?

JUST BECAUSE THEY'RE IMPORTANT DOESN'T MEAN YOU NEED TO KEEP THEM IN IMPRESSIVE FILES. IT'S BEST TO SIMPLIFY WHEN YOU CAN.

I THOUGHT I HAD TO STORE THIS FOR LIFE IN A REALLY STURDY FILE...

THIS IS SO THIN!

CATEGORY THREE, "OTHER"...

...IS EVERY-THING ELSE BESIDES ONE AND TWO.

THIS MEANS PAPERS YOU USE FAIRLY FREQUENTLY

BUT THAT YOU DON'T NEED TO SAVE AS LONG AS CONTRACTS.

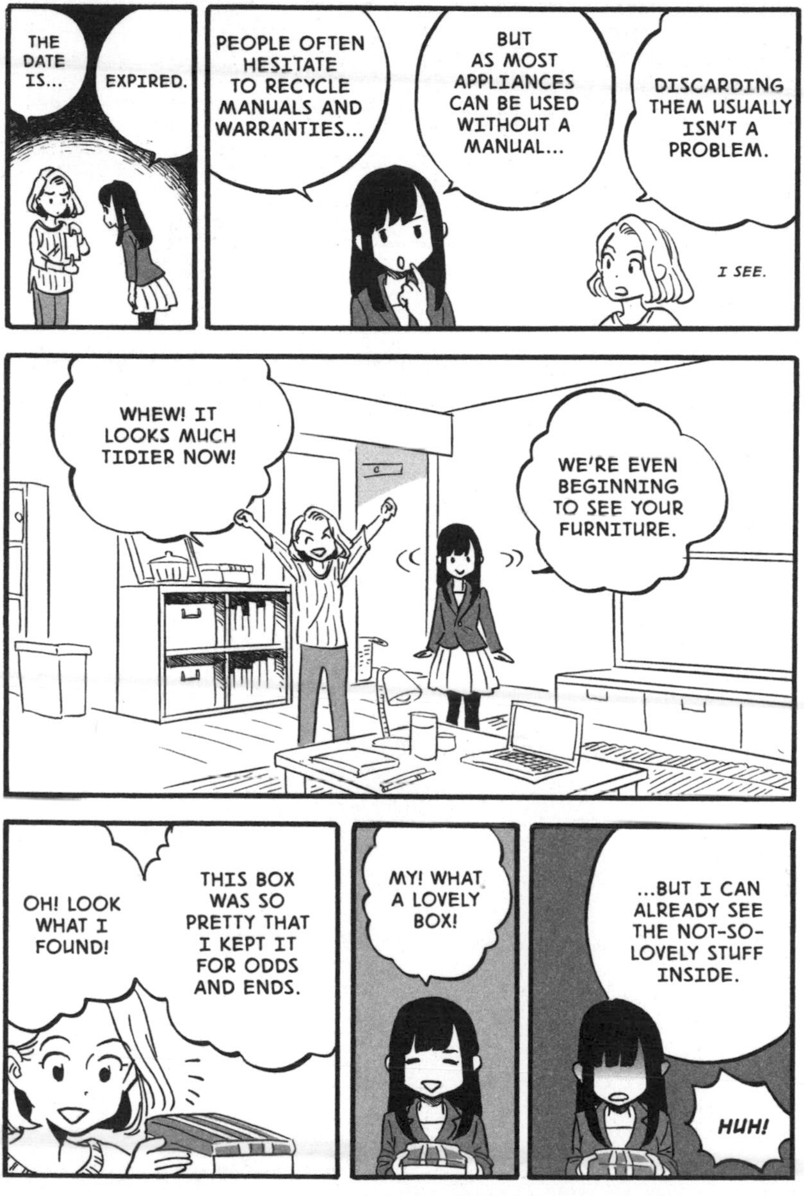
THE DATE IS...
EXPIRED.
PEOPLE OFTEN HESITATE TO RECYCLE MANUALS AND WARRANTIES...
BUT AS MOST APPLIANCES CAN BE USED WITHOUT A MANUAL...
DISCARDING THEM USUALLY ISN'T A PROBLEM.
I SEE.
WHEW! IT LOOKS MUCH TIDIER NOW!
WE'RE EVEN BEGINNING TO SEE YOUR FURNITURE.
OH! LOOK WHAT I FOUND!
THIS BOX WAS SO PRETTY THAT I KEPT IT FOR ODDS AND ENDS.
MY! WHAT A LOVELY BOX!
...BUT I CAN ALREADY SEE THE NOT-SO-LOVELY STUFF INSIDE.
HUH!

WRISTWATCH BAND PIECE

NOVELTY POST-ITS

KEY RINGS
(...NEVER USED...)

TWO-YEAR OLD DATEBOOK
(UNUSED)

Hawaii

HOKKAIDO

RUSTY HAIRPINS

LEFTOVER MEDICINE

BATTERIES
(USED... ?)

USED ERASER BITS

A STICKY BALLPOINT PEN

NO JOY!!

COINS

COINS ARE MONEY, TOO, BUT COMPARED TO BILLS THEY'RE TREATED VERY CALLOUSLY, AREN'T THEY?

FROM NOW ON, WHEN YOU SEE SMALL CHANGE...

MAKE "INTO MY WALLET" YOUR MOTTO.

KEEP THOSE WORDS IN MIND AND RESCUE ANY POOR COINS YOU FIND AS YOU TIDY.

ONE, TWO, THREE... THERE SURE ARE A LOT.

IN!!

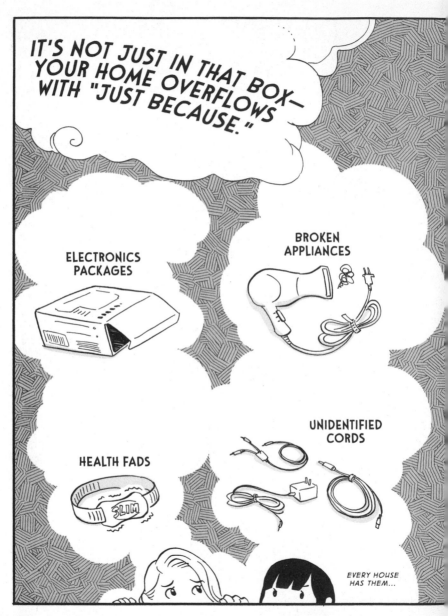

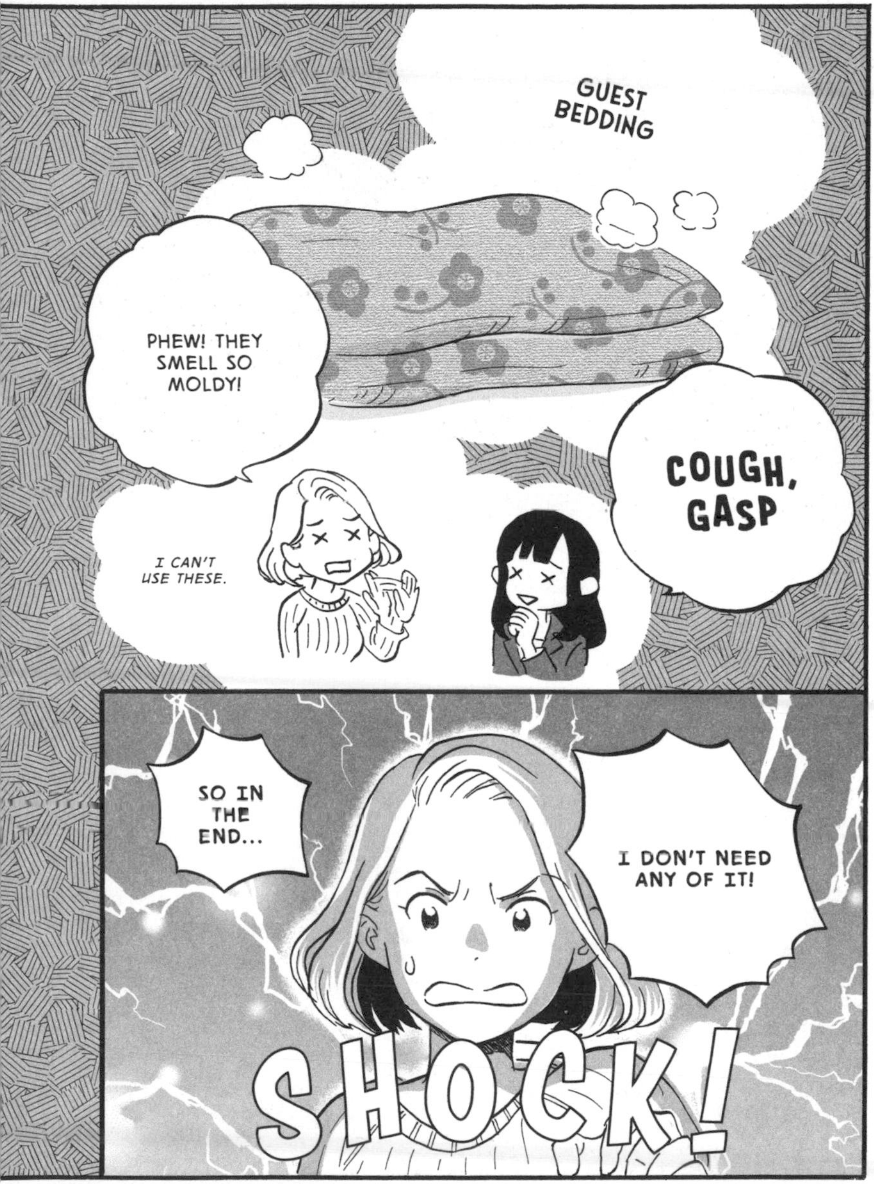
GUEST BEDDING
PHEW! THEY SMELL SO MOLDY!
COUGH, GASP
I CAN'T USE THESE.
SO IN THE END...
I DON'T NEED ANY OF IT!
SHOCK!

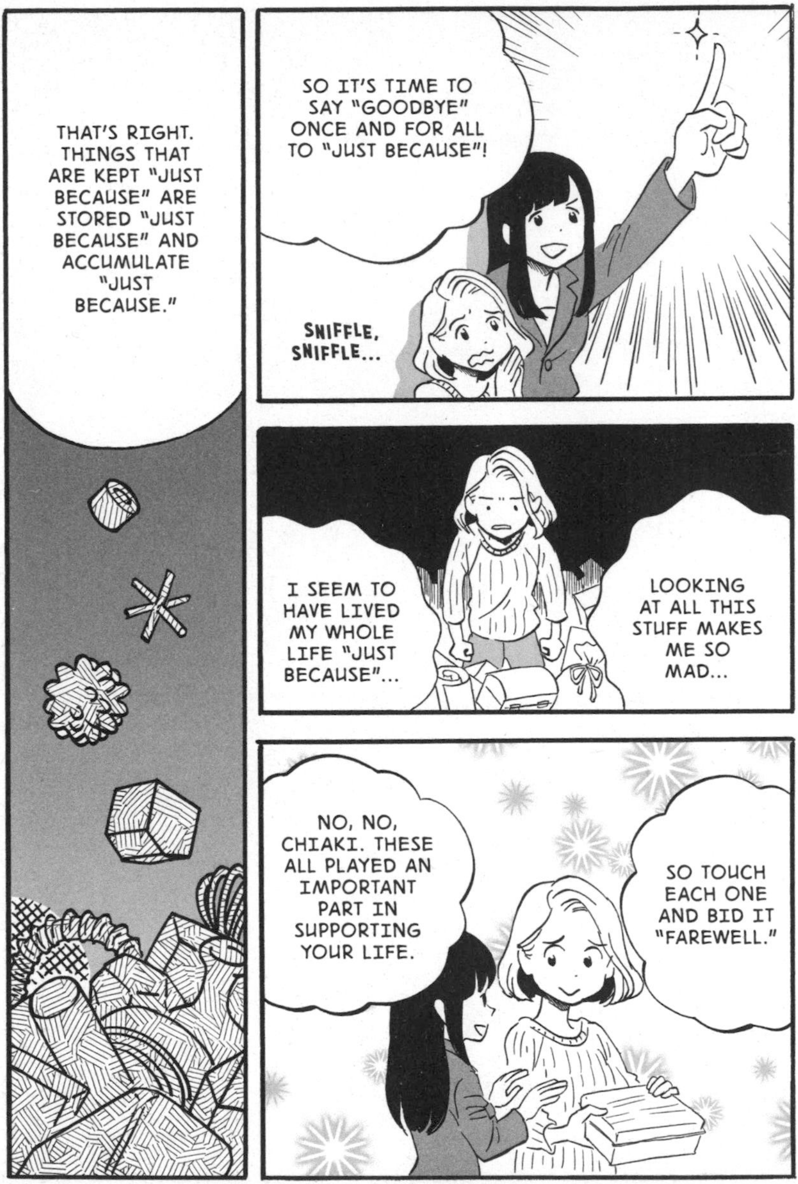
THAT'S RIGHT. THINGS THAT ARE KEPT "JUST BECAUSE" ARE STORED "JUST BECAUSE" AND ACCUMULATE "JUST BECAUSE."
SO IT'S TIME TO SAY "GOODBYE" ONCE AND FOR ALL TO "JUST BECAUSE"!
SNIFFLE, SNIFFLE...
I SEEM TO HAVE LIVED MY WHOLE LIFE "JUST BECAUSE"...
LOOKING AT ALL THIS STUFF MAKES ME SO MAD...
NO, NO, CHIAKI. THESE ALL PLAYED AN IMPORTANT PART IN SUPPORTING YOUR LIFE.
SO TOUCH EACH ONE AND BID IT "FAREWELL."

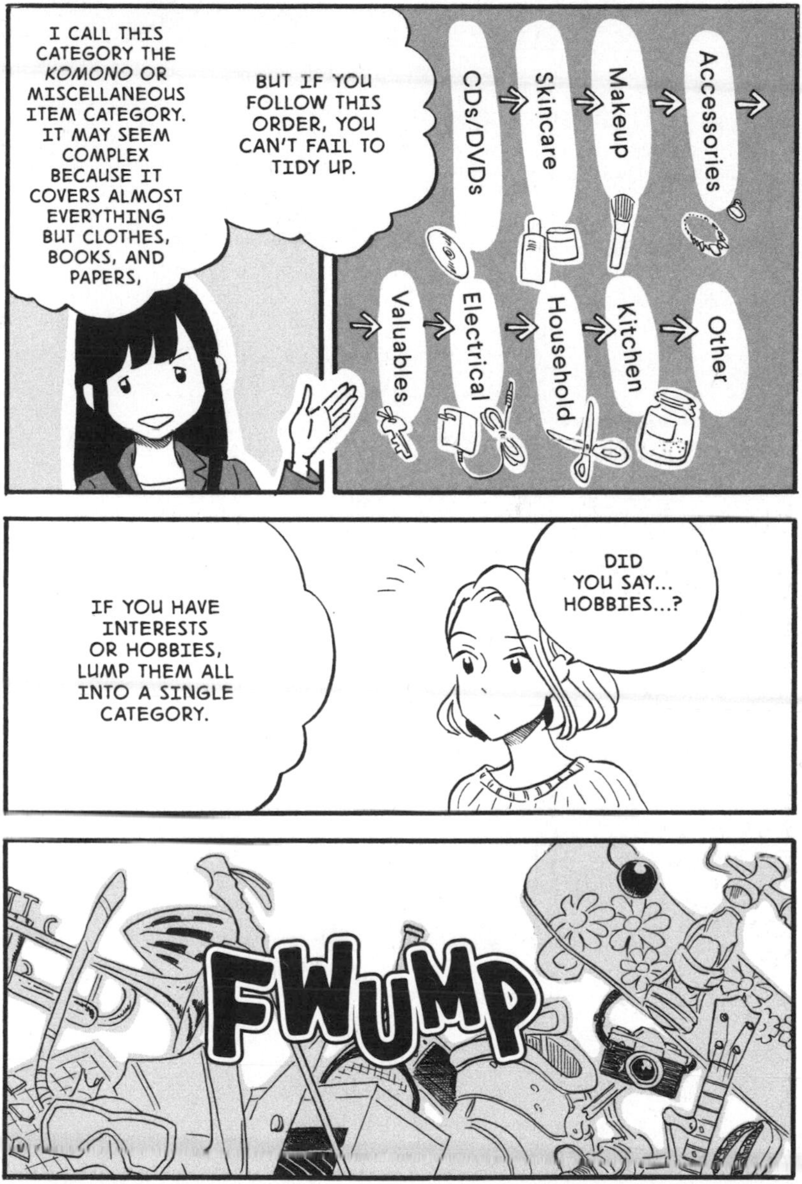

I CALL THIS CATEGORY THE *KOMONO* OR MISCELLANEOUS ITEM CATEGORY. IT MAY SEEM COMPLEX BECAUSE IT COVERS ALMOST EVERYTHING BUT CLOTHES, BOOKS, AND PAPERS,
BUT IF YOU FOLLOW THIS ORDER, YOU CAN'T FAIL TO TIDY UP.
CDs/DVDs
Skincare
Makeup
Accessories
Valuables
Electrical
Household
Kitchen
Other
IF YOU HAVE INTERESTS OR HOBBIES, LUMP THEM ALL INTO A SINGLE CATEGORY.
DID YOU SAY... HOBBIES...?
FWUMP

The rule of thumb for papers is to discard them all. Keep only those that you're certain you will use in the future.

———

Discard any papers that don't fall into one of the following three categories: those you are currently using, those you will need for a limited period of time, and those that you need to keep indefinitely.

Put all those papers that require action, such as letters you need to respond to or bills you need to pay, in a "Pending" box, set a date for dealing with them, and tackle them all in one go. Unfinished business like this weighs on the mind far more than we realize. You'll feel much better if you get this job out of the way quickly.

8

leave
sentimental
items
for last

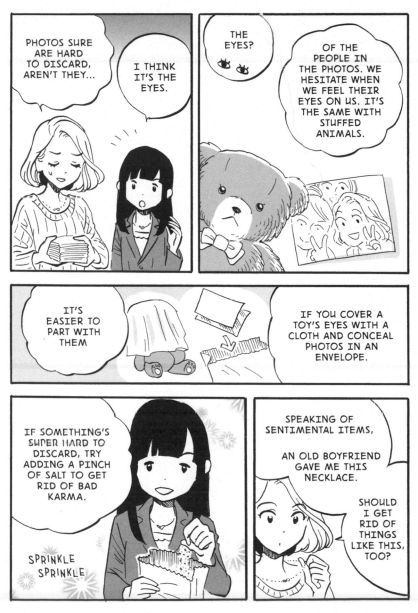

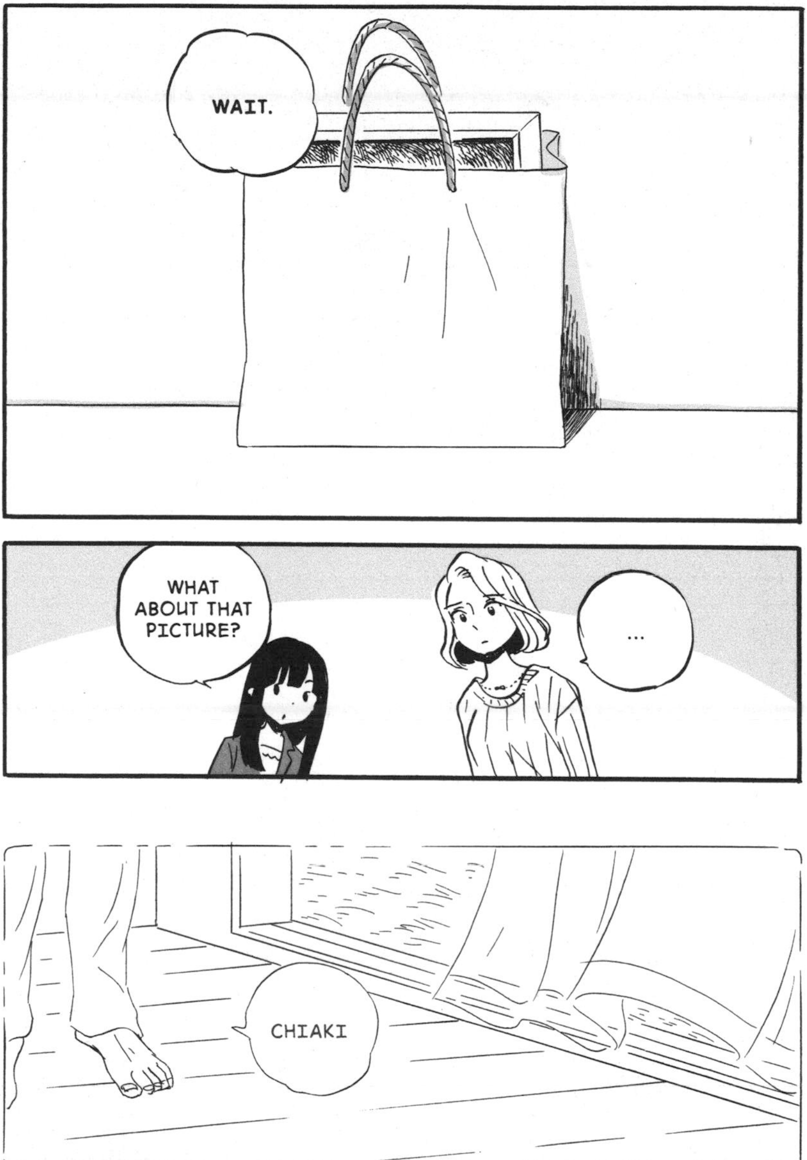
WAIT.
WHAT ABOUT THAT PICTURE?
...
CHIAKI

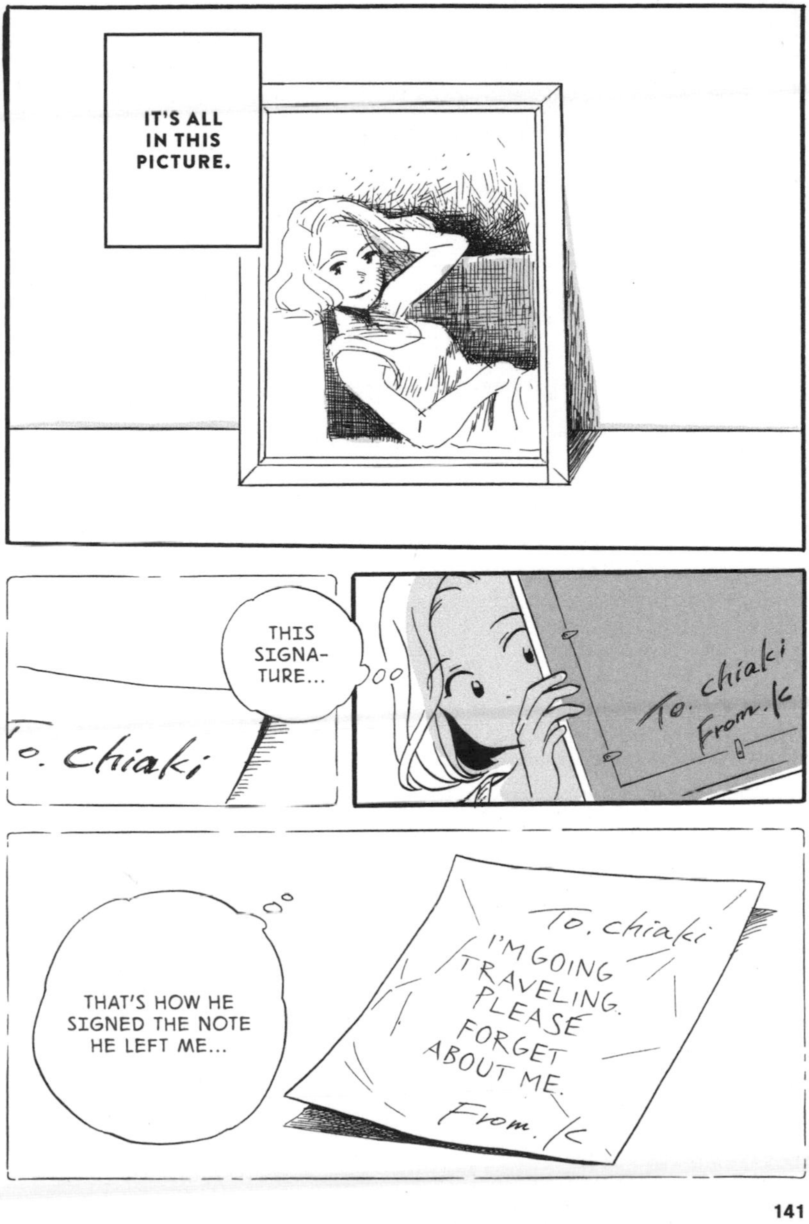
IT'S ALL IN THIS PICTURE.
o. chiaki
THIS SIGNA-TURE...
To. chiaki
From. K
THAT'S HOW HE SIGNED THE NOTE HE LEFT ME...
To. chiaki
I'M GOING TRAVELING. PLEASE FORGET ABOUT ME.
From. K

OH NO! THE GARBAGE TRUCK!

WAIT! WAIT! MORE TRASH!

TH-THANK YOU! I'M SO GLAD YOU STOPPED HIM.

NO, I'M SORRY FOR BEHAVING LIKE THAT.

BUT THANKS TO YOU, I FEEL LIKE I CAN MOVE FORWARD NOW.

I THOUGHT IT WAS MY FAULT THAT YOU DIDN'T GET TO THROW IT OUT LAST NIGHT.

SORRY FOR BEING SO INSEN- SITIVE.

thump- thump

WHAT DID YOU THROW AWAY?

IT'S A SECRET.

We live in this moment. Who you are now is more important than memories of your past. Be good to yourself.

―――――

It is so hard to let go of things that once brought us joy and are filled with precious memories. It feels like we are losing the memories along with them. But that is not the case. Memories that are truly precious will never be forgotten, even if we discard an item associated with them.

What really matters is not the past but the person we have now become, thanks to those past experiences. We should use our space not for the person we once were, but for our future selves.

9 store things where they belong

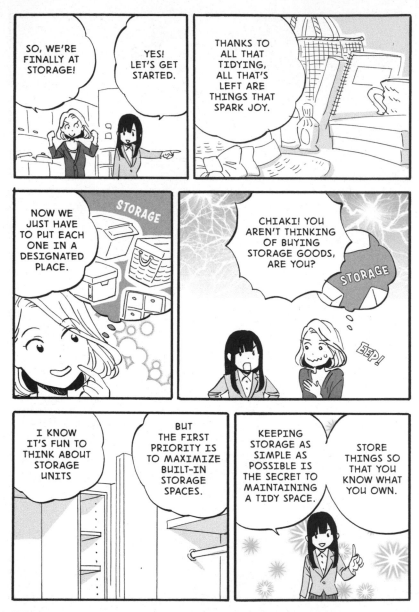

SO, WE'RE FINALLY AT STORAGE!

YES! LET'S GET STARTED.

THANKS TO ALL THAT TIDYING, ALL THAT'S LEFT ARE THINGS THAT SPARK JOY.

NOW WE JUST HAVE TO PUT EACH ONE IN A DESIGNATED PLACE.

STORAGE

CHIAKI! YOU AREN'T THINKING OF BUYING STORAGE GOODS, ARE YOU?

STORAGE

EEP!

I KNOW IT'S FUN TO THINK ABOUT STORAGE UNITS

BUT THE FIRST PRIORITY IS TO MAXIMIZE BUILT-IN STORAGE SPACES.

KEEPING STORAGE AS SIMPLE AS POSSIBLE IS THE SECRET TO MAINTAINING A TIDY SPACE.

STORE THINGS SO THAT YOU KNOW WHAT YOU OWN.

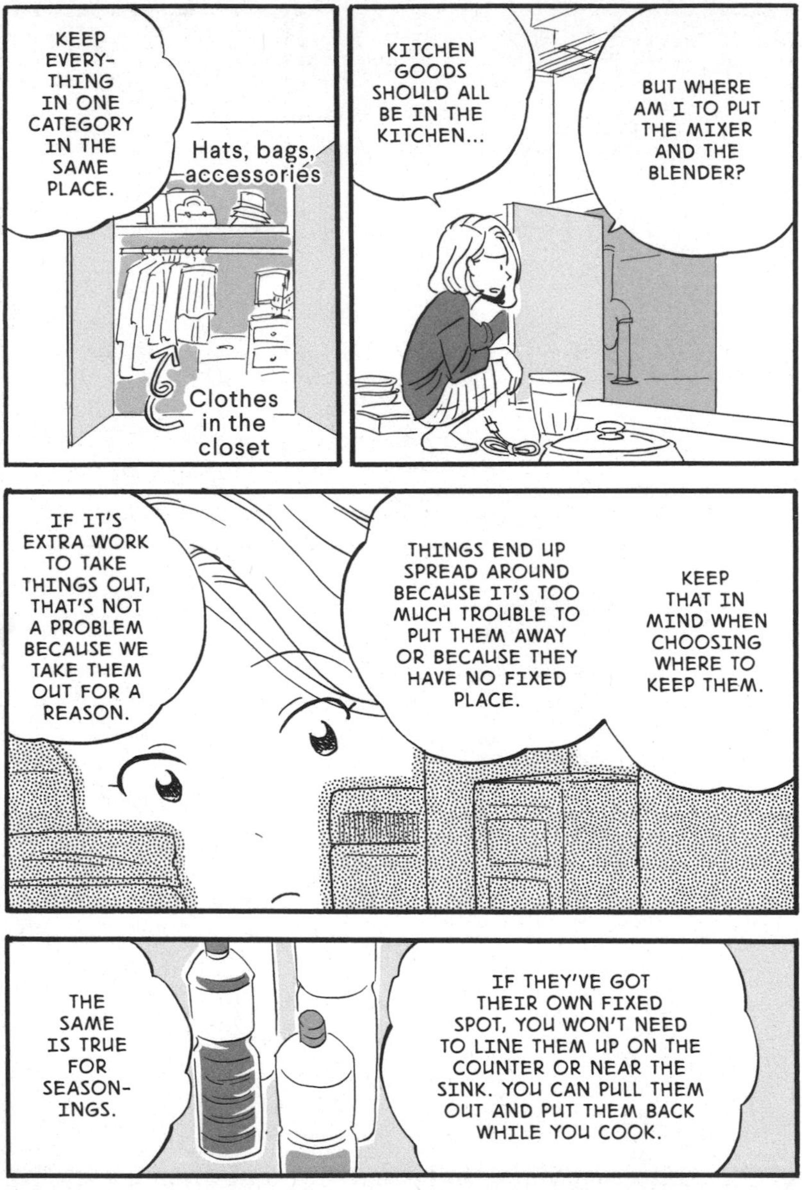
KEEP EVERY-THING IN ONE CATEGORY IN THE SAME PLACE.
Hats, bags, accessories
Clothes in the closet
KITCHEN GOODS SHOULD ALL BE IN THE KITCHEN...
BUT WHERE AM I TO PUT THE MIXER AND THE BLENDER?
IF IT'S EXTRA WORK TO TAKE THINGS OUT, THAT'S NOT A PROBLEM BECAUSE WE TAKE THEM OUT FOR A REASON.
THINGS END UP SPREAD AROUND BECAUSE IT'S TOO MUCH TROUBLE TO PUT THEM AWAY OR BECAUSE THEY HAVE NO FIXED PLACE.
KEEP THAT IN MIND WHEN CHOOSING WHERE TO KEEP THEM.
THE SAME IS TRUE FOR SEASON-INGS.
IF THEY'VE GOT THEIR OWN FIXED SPOT, YOU WON'T NEED TO LINE THEM UP ON THE COUNTER OR NEAR THE SINK. YOU CAN PULL THEM OUT AND PUT THEM BACK WHILE YOU COOK.

STOCKINGS

TOILETRIES

YOU CAN USE SHOEBOXES FOR SO MUCH MORE!

USE THE LID LIKE A TRAY

OF COURSE, IT DOESN'T HAVE TO BE SHOEBOXES.

DURING THE TIDYING PROCESS, JUST USE WHAT YOU'VE GOT IN THE HOUSE.

SQUARE CONTAINERS WORK BETTER THAN ROUND OR IRREGULARLY SHAPED ONES.

INSTEAD OF BUYING STORAGE GOODS TO MAKE DO, WAIT UNTIL YOU'VE COMPLETELY FINISHED AND LOOK FOR ONES YOU REALLY LIKE.

YOU MEAN DON'T BUY THINGS "JUST BECAUSE"!

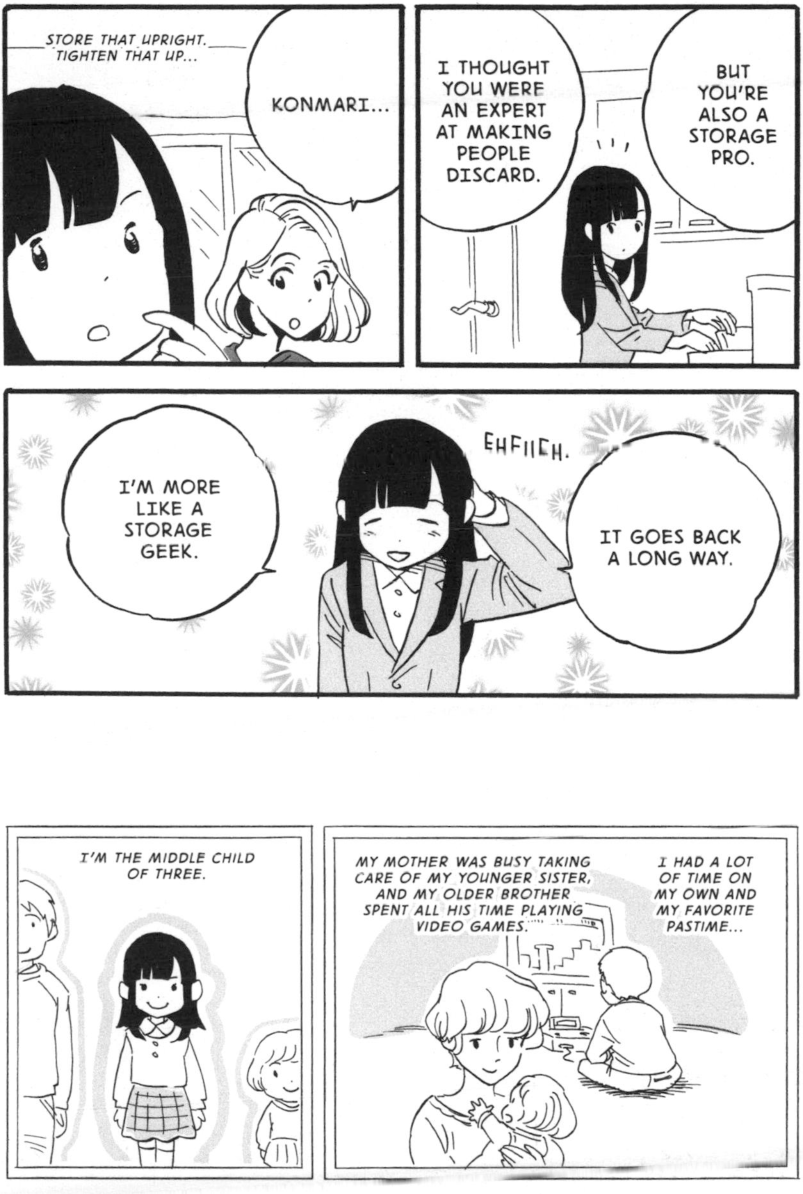
STORE THAT UPRIGHT. TIGHTEN THAT UP...
KONMARI...
I THOUGHT YOU WERE AN EXPERT AT MAKING PEOPLE DISCARD.
BUT YOU'RE ALSO A STORAGE PRO.
I'M MORE LIKE A STORAGE GEEK.
IT GOES BACK A LONG WAY.
I'M THE MIDDLE CHILD OF THREE.
MY MOTHER WAS BUSY TAKING CARE OF MY YOUNGER SISTER, AND MY OLDER BROTHER SPENT ALL HIS TIME PLAYING VIDEO GAMES.
I HAD A LOT OF TIME ON MY OWN AND MY FAVORITE PASTIME...

WAS TO READ LIFESTYLE MAGAZINES.

TIDY UP

FOR GOOD!

55 storage tips

IN ELEMENTARY SCHOOL, I LIKED TIDYING UP THE BOOKS IN THE BOOKCASE

AND COMPLAINING ABOUT THE ORGANIZATION OF THE BROOM CLOSET.

toss toss

toss toss

IN JUNIOR HIGH, I BECAME SERIOUS ABOUT TIDYING.

I'VE ACCUMULATED TOO MUCH STUFF!

AFTER A WEEK OF TIDYING, MY ROOM WAS TRANSFORMED, AND I FELT AS IF I HAD BEEN STRUCK BY LIGHTNING.

TIDYING, I SUDDENLY REALIZED, WAS A MUCH GREATER ACT THAN I HAD EVER IMAGINED.

SO THAT'S HOW YOU REACHED THE PINNACLE OF TIDYING UP!

BUT ONLY THROUGH CONTINUOUS TRIAL AND ERROR.

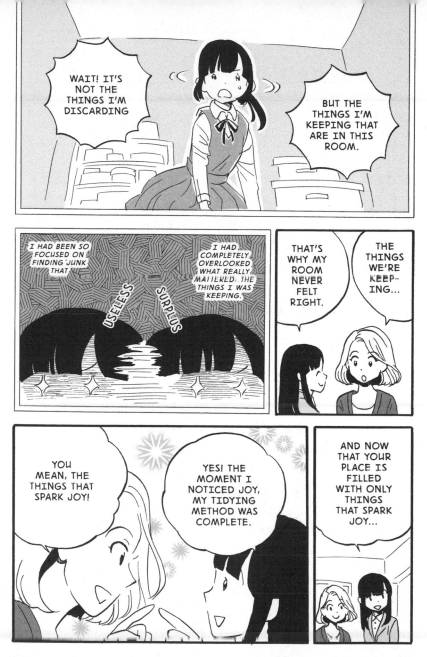

WAIT! IT'S NOT THE THINGS I'M DISCARDING

BUT THE THINGS I'M KEEPING THAT ARE IN THIS ROOM.

I HAD BEEN SO COMPLETELY FOCUSED ON FINDING JUNK THAT...

USELESS

SURPLUS

I HAD COMPLETELY OVERLOOKED WHAT REALLY MATTERED: THE THINGS I WAS KEEPING.

THAT'S WHY MY ROOM NEVER FELT RIGHT.

THE THINGS WE'RE KEEP-ING...

YOU MEAN, THE THINGS THAT SPARK JOY!

YES! THE MOMENT I NOTICED JOY, MY TIDYING METHOD WAS COMPLETE.

AND NOW THAT YOUR PLACE IS FILLED WITH ONLY THINGS THAT SPARK JOY...

164

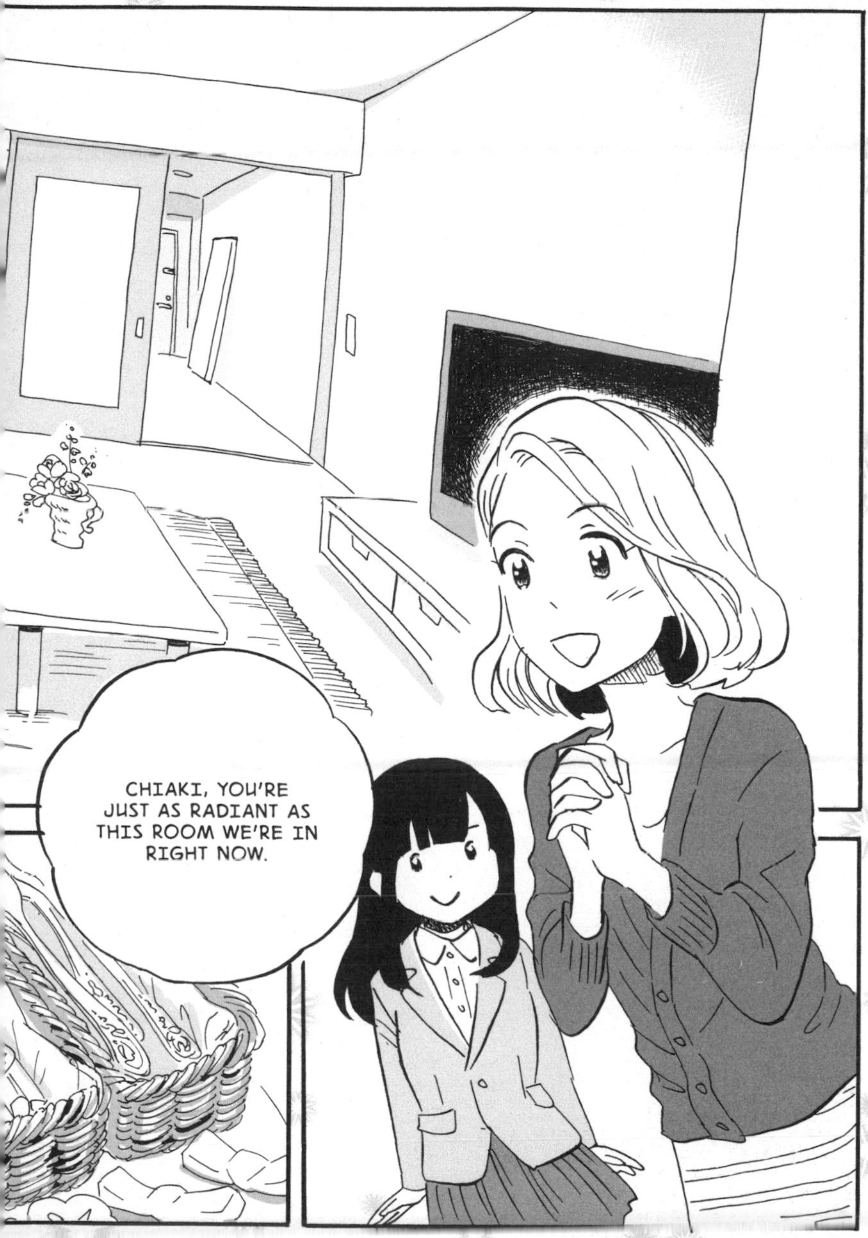
CHIAKI, YOU'RE JUST AS RADIANT AS THIS ROOM WE'RE IN RIGHT NOW.

Designate a "home" for each thing and store it where it belongs.

———

Although we may not be aware of it, our belongings work hard to support us every day. Just as we like to come home and relax after a long day's work, our things breathe a sigh of relief when they are returned to where they belong. It's very important to give our things the security of having a place to come home to.

Things that are returned each day to their designated place are different. They have a special glow. If we take good care of our possessions, they will take good care of us.

real life
begins after
putting
your house
in order

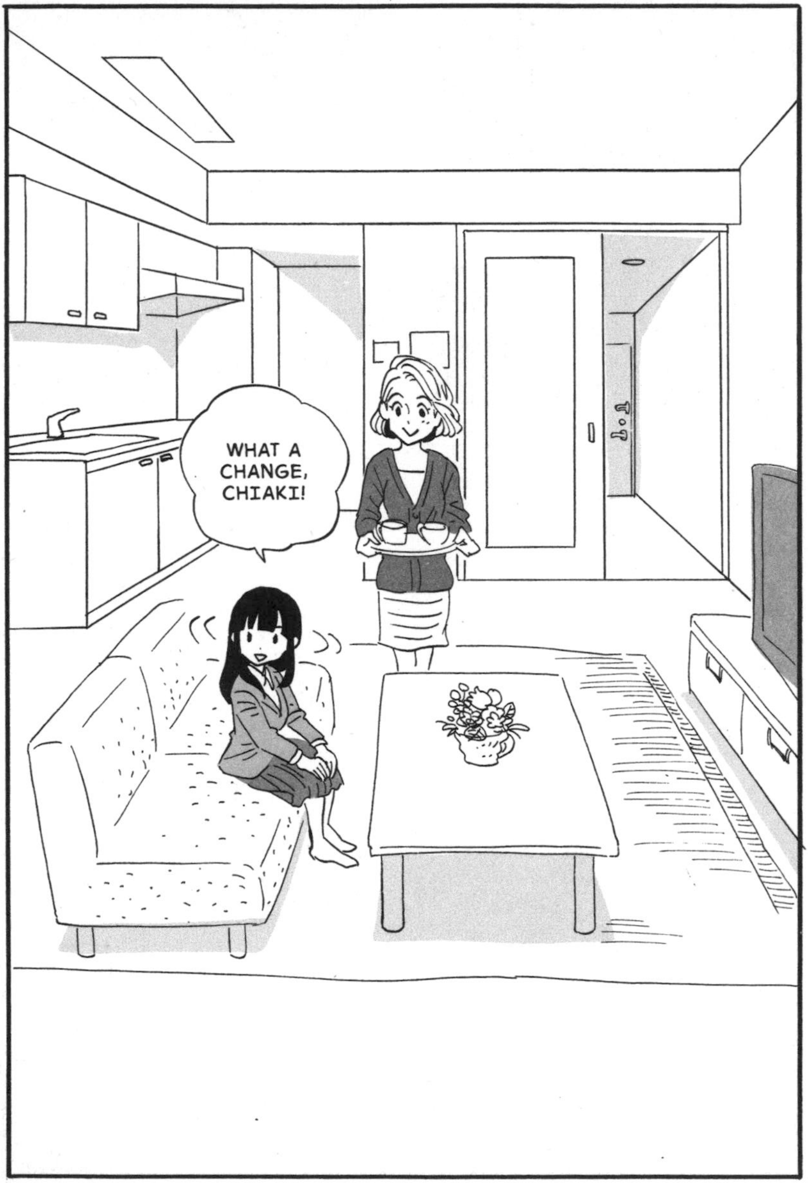
WHAT A CHANGE, CHIAKI!

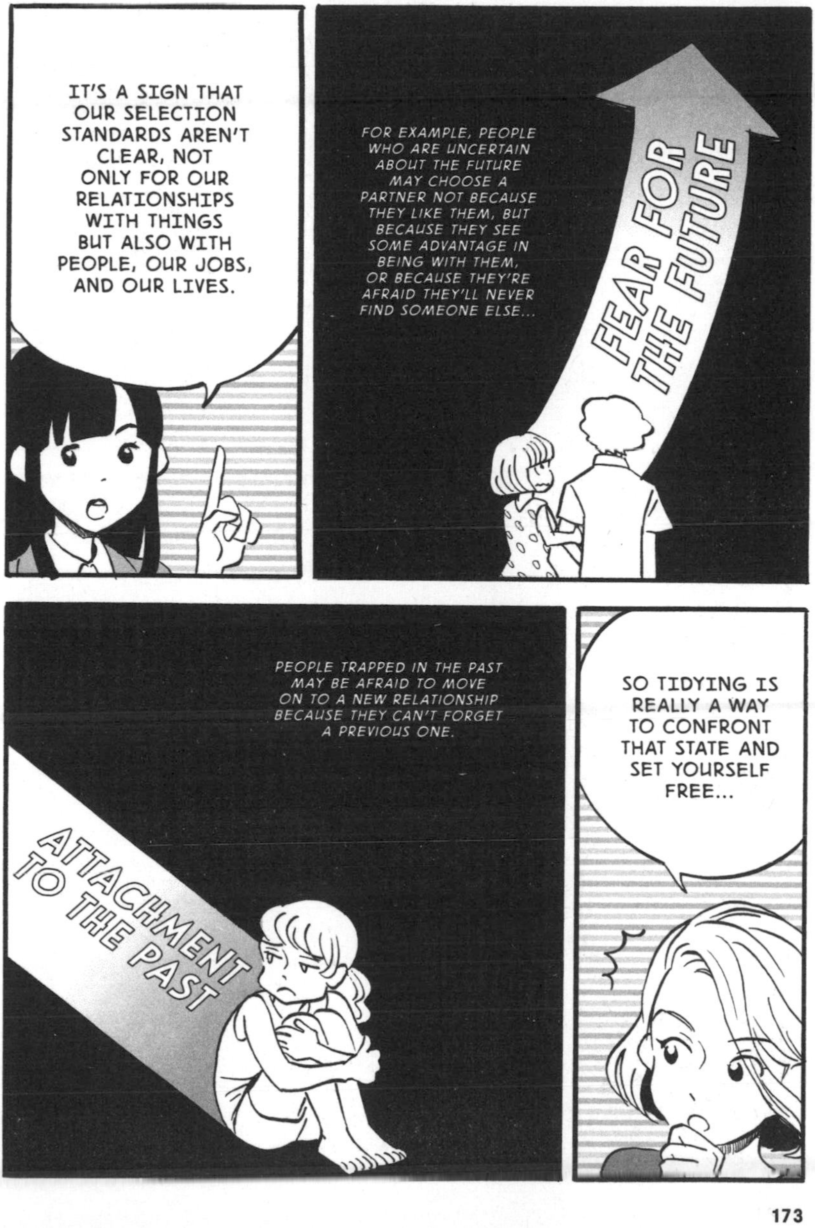
IT'S A SIGN THAT OUR SELECTION STANDARDS AREN'T CLEAR, NOT ONLY FOR OUR RELATIONSHIPS WITH THINGS BUT ALSO WITH PEOPLE, OUR JOBS, AND OUR LIVES.
FOR EXAMPLE, PEOPLE WHO ARE UNCERTAIN ABOUT THE FUTURE MAY CHOOSE A PARTNER NOT BECAUSE THEY LIKE THEM, BUT BECAUSE THEY SEE SOME ADVANTAGE IN BEING WITH THEM, OR BECAUSE THEY'RE AFRAID THEY'LL NEVER FIND SOMEONE ELSE...
FEAR FOR THE FUTURE
PEOPLE TRAPPED IN THE PAST MAY BE AFRAID TO MOVE ON TO A NEW RELATIONSHIP BECAUSE THEY CAN'T FORGET A PREVIOUS ONE.
ATTACHMENT TO THE PAST
SO TIDYING IS REALLY A WAY TO CONFRONT THAT STATE AND SET YOURSELF FREE...

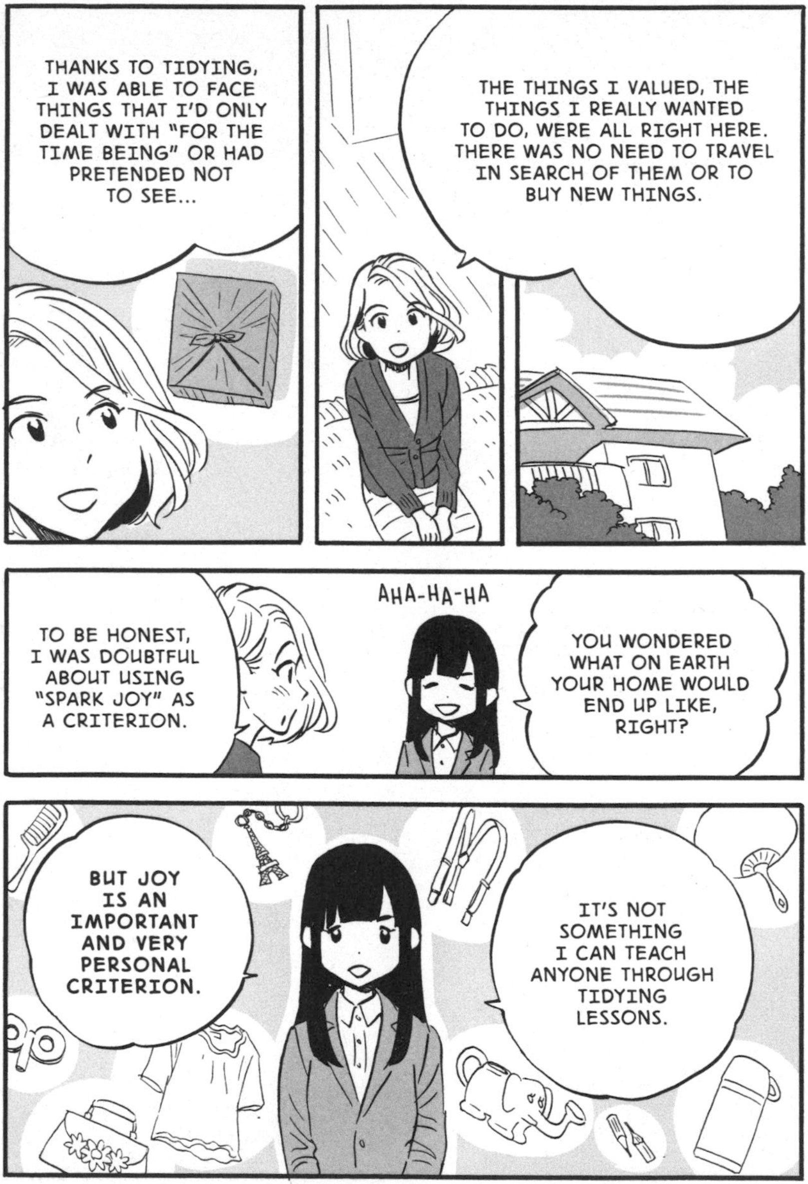
THANKS TO TIDYING, I WAS ABLE TO FACE THINGS THAT I'D ONLY DEALT WITH "FOR THE TIME BEING" OR HAD PRETENDED NOT TO SEE...
THE THINGS I VALUED, THE THINGS I REALLY WANTED TO DO, WERE ALL RIGHT HERE. THERE WAS NO NEED TO TRAVEL IN SEARCH OF THEM OR TO BUY NEW THINGS.
TO BE HONEST, I WAS DOUBTFUL ABOUT USING "SPARK JOY" AS A CRITERION.
AHA-HA-HA
YOU WONDERED WHAT ON EARTH YOUR HOME WOULD END UP LIKE, RIGHT?
BUT JOY IS AN IMPORTANT AND VERY PERSONAL CRITERION.
IT'S NOT SOMETHING I CAN TEACH ANYONE THROUGH TIDYING LESSONS.

179

afterword

As a tidying consultant, I have seen how tidying up sparks joy in the lives of many people.

Work, relationships, falling in love . . . the magic of tidying up positively impacts every aspect of life.

If you want to spark more joy in your life, try tidying up by following the advice in this manga. The effect will be even greater than you expect.

I hope that through tidying you will experience joy in your life every day.